# THE UNMUTING

by

## Osamu Hashizu
## "Sam"

First Edition, October 2022, manufactured in USA
1 2 3 4 5 6 7 8 9 10  LSI 22 23 24 25 26
Set in Copperplate, Minion Pro and Times Roman

ISBN: 979-8-9873789-0-8

Front cover photograph by Josh Kameyer

*"There is nothing outside of yourself that can ever enable you*

*to get better, stronger, richer, quicker, or smarter.*

*Everything is within.*

*Everything exists.*

*Seek nothing outside of yourself."*

Miyamoto Musashi

Dedicated to my family

and my friends old and new,

to discover where and what I come from

and the ancestral lineage my children come from,

to learn the process and the journey I have traveled,

to understand the spiritual principles that have guided me,

to be inspired to create a better life than what you think you can,

to believe in yourself and know that you are greater than you think you are,

and to realize how to laugh, be calm, be you, and allow the universe to support you.

To know what it means to be a part of this honorable lineage might change the attitudes

you have about yourself and about life and help you to understand why people of other

cultures have always respected the way the Japanese conduct themselves.

How you react to this information and what you do with it

all depend on how you interpret and digest it.

May you gain a sense of inner strength.

But, the decisions you make

and the journeys you take

are yours to choose.

# CONTENTS

# FOREWORD

I started reading *The Unmuting* one evening on my way to bed and forgot all about time. Engaging, stimulating, and adventurous, it had me looking in the mirror, evaluating my deepest beliefs, and considering the direction of my life's path.

Sam's innocent, open manner shines through each page and story of his dynamic life, including the ups and downs and successes and failures. From hot cars and crazy road trips to overcoming addictive behaviors, *The Unmuting* is the unvarnished truth about the events that shaped the man I've come to call my friend. Once you begin Sam's journey, you won't want to stop. Enjoy the ride. I did.

As a business coach to CEOs and executives, I serve highly successful lawyers and accountants from the big four firms. Sam's bright intelligence, business acumen, and superior knowledge of finance, business, and tax are equal to any of them. However, his standard of excellence, responsiveness, and conscientious, caring attitude make him a breed apart.

Sam Hashizu is at the top of his game and more than ready and able to serve you. Take the opportunity to allow him to do just that.

David Rohlander
Author of *The CEO Code*

# INTRODUCTION

*"Two of the greatest gifts we can give our*

*children are roots and wings."*

Dennis Waitley

Like Kunta Kinte in *Roots*, I wanted to know where I came from. My mother and father had never talked about our ancestry, so I didn't know anything until about ten years ago. I've shared a little of what I discovered with my nephews and nieces, but most people know nothing about my Samurai ancestry, not even my kids—*until now.*

About ten years ago, my uncle began telling me about his trips to Japan and how he had set up meetings with Buddhist monks because they were the only people who could translate the fourteenth-century scroll he had retrieved from his uncle. It was the original calligraphy penned scroll upon which each Samurai wrote his bio before passing it down to the next generation's Samurai.

The more my uncle shared with me, the more curious I became. When I bought a genealogy book, to my surprise, I was able to trace our family lineage all the way back to the first emperor of Japan. Myth tells that the first emperor was born from the left eye of the Sun Goddess in Heaven. Each succeeding emperor was a blood descendant of the first. My mother's maiden name, Kono, was our Samurai name and dated back to the beginning of time.

Kono was the captain of the ship of men who fought the Chinese invading Japan.

I had not been back to my birthplace of Shimane-Ken since my family moved when I was two. So, in 2012, I took my first trip back with my mom. We visited the local museum where I saw our Mon, the family crest, showcased in glass. Picture taking was prohibited inside, but I *had* to have the Mon in my possession, so I took a snapshot.

My uncle had been to Shimane-Ken to visit his nephews (my cousins) and had introduced us through email, but I'd never met them or any of my relatives in Japan. In 2019, I took a solo journey back. I didn't tell them I was coming. I just showed up and knocked on the door and said, *"Hi I'm Osamu Hashizu, your cousin."* They took me in and showed me their home, then drove me to the home I had lived in when I was born. The door was open, so I went inside and took some photographs. It was fairly large and beautiful and had a gorgeous rice patty in the front. The neighbors told us that the house had been abandoned for about four years.

We visited the nearby Samurai grave site, which my family has been taking care of since the fourteenth century. I saw our family "Mon" engraved on some of the headstones. Along with the photo of our Mon, today I have all of the documentation of our Samurai lineage and other artifacts, like Samurai spears and pictures of the first Kono family.

Like the Samurai, the Japanese are extremely honorable. Their word is solid and can always be trusted. They work in a meditative state of mind, free from distractions and maintain a state of inner serenity. This is called, *The Way of the Samurai*, or *Bushido*, which means acting with honor, respect, and integrity, in meditation and serenity, and emotionless.

*The Way of the Samurai* is reflected in the Samurai warrior battles. The code of Bushido dictates that the Samurai must honor his opponent in battle, which is exemplified in the famous historical Samurai fight to the death. After killing his opponent in the duel, the Samurai neglected to pay compliments to his defeated opponent. In dishonoring his opponent, he dishonored himself and his hundred disciples watching, and they all committed suicide.

The Samurai suicide is a gruesome, but honorable one, facilitated by first piercing the stomach with a short sword and then horizontally slicing it. The Japanese believe that the stomach holds the person's chi energy, their identity. To prevent their chi from being stolen by anyone, they sliced the stomach to allow the chi to spill out of the body. Immediately afterwards, to eliminate suffering and expedite his death, a disciple or other designated person cuts his head off.

Though the era of the Samurai has passed, Japanese culture carries the Bushido way within its ancestral lineage, including its language. Much like the lack of emotion displayed in *The Way of the Samurai*, the Japanese language is spoken monotone, with no accented syllables or sentences. There is no emotional emphasis. Unlike the English language, where some letters are silent, every letter in the Japanese language makes a sound. Unlike the Chinese language, which contains sound changes that alter the meaning of words, each letter in the Japanese language makes only one sound. It is unshifting. This emotionless way of behavior and speech is carried within the DNA of every Japanese descendant.

To my children and relatives, you may be wondering why I'm mentioning the language and letters. The pride and emotional restraint in *The Way of the Samurai* greatly affected my personality from birth through most of my life, as you will soon find out. My mother had approximately twenty-five grandchildren and great-grandchildren, *which include you*. Even though I may not appear to act this way now, it was very much a part of the foundation that I came from. And you are part of this Samurai lineage. You carry this mentality and Bushido way within your DNA and familial influence.

What you do with this influence and information is up to you. One of my nephew's sons adopted the nickname "Kono Joe" and had it sewn into his wrestler's jacket. I'm sure that was inspired by his dad's sharing with him the history of our powerful Samurai lineage. Most likely, it made a difference in his mindset and the energy he competes with. I believe that knowing your ancestry won't put you on an ego trip or cause you to expect others to respect you or treat you better than others. You can choose to internalize the esteem and honor of our family heritage and receive inner strength from it, without feeling the need to tell everyone. But, I have no expectations of you. The choice and journey are for each of you to decide for yourselves.

# Chapter 1

# Childhood

# The Trauma Journey

*"Be patient.*

*Every seed we plant requires a period of*

*incubation before it manifests."*

Unknown

My Mom was born in Los Angeles, California, and grew up on a farm. Before World War II, my mom returned to Shimane-Ken, Japan to take care of her father. It was there that she met and married my father in a pre-arranged union. They gave birth to my two sisters, and then I arrived on the scene on February 23, 1947. We moved to Hiroshima, Japan, when I was two years old.

In Japanese culture at that time, the husband's role was the breadwinner and provider for the family. He handed his paychecks to his wife, who handled the household expenses and maintenance and raised the children. Typically, the husband worked ten or twelve-hour days, seven days a week, after which he stayed out late fraternizing with his buddies. This left little time to spend with his wife and children. This was my dad to a T.

I would describe his presence as muted. He didn't speak much and engaged with me on the sideline, meaning that he didn't get involved in the day-to-day affairs of raising his children. He didn't meddle or give any instructions. My mom did all of that, while he observed. My dad lost his temper with my mother only once. He was more protective than she was and never told my sisters or me what to do or how to be. I recall only one major incident between us during a period when he worked from home as a collector and seller of odds and ends. I was seven and had taken a very heavy anvil off one of his shelves and dropped it. I didn't hurt myself, but my dad became really upset with me for putting myself in harm's way and told me that I needed to be more careful so I wouldn't injure myself.

In World War II, my dad was a Morse code operator on a Japanese naval ship. Upon landing on a desolate island, his commanding officer asked for a few volunteers to stay on the island while the ship sailed to its next destination. My dad volunteered. The island was barren of food, animals, and vegetation, and he and the others survived on a diet of rats and insects. A month after departing, his ship was bombed and sank to the bottom of the ocean. There were no survivors. When I heard this story, I understood why my dad had always been so quiet and in control of his temper.

The culture during the time we lived in Hiroshima dictated that children were quiet and didn't talk. My mother exemplified *The Way of the Samurai*. Strong and strict, she wore the pants. She wanted me to be independent and imprinted on me that I didn't need anything from anybody and could take care of myself. I remember one of my uncles offering money to me one time. I told him that I didn't want to take his money from him. My mom was very proud of me for that.

She was not a compassionate person, but rather forceful and demanding. Her remedy for my colds or flu was to make me eat a live garden snail. She put sugar on top of it as if that would make it palatable. I can still remember the taste and the sound. The first bite was always the worst, that large, awful squish, as the entire guts exploded into the recesses of my mouth. At bath time, I took an *ofuro*. Before getting into the tub, I stood next to it and washed my entire body with soap and a washcloth. After that, I got into the tub to wash again and rinse off the layers of soap. The water in the tub was boiling hot and steaming and extremely painful to my tender young skin. She forced me to get in with her unspoken words, *"Just take it like a man."*

One of the most painful experiences of my childhood was breaking my leg on the playground. I was taken to the hospital, but Japanese doctors didn't use anaesthesia back then. They ended up resetting it wrong, so I was sent to a bone specialist who pulled my leg bones apart to unhinge them and reset them again.

The worst pain of my childhood was having appendicitis. I was seven. With no anaesthesia, I was not put to sleep or given any pain killer. After a simple shot to numb the skin of the area, I lay awake through the entire surgery incisions and removal of my appendix. I remember my mom telling me afterwards not to put pressure on my stomach, because my intestines were popping out and had to be put back inside of me.

Fortunately, by the time I needed to have my tonsils removed, we had moved to the US where the world was civilized and doctors used anaesthesia. My two older sisters were not so lucky, as we still lived in Japan when their tonsils were removed with just a local numbing shot.

My auntie and my uncle sponsored our family's immigration to the United States when I was eight, and we sailed in a boat with a couple of hundred people from Japan to San Francisco, California. From there, we went to Oasis, California, to live on my uncle's farm. Our house was fifty feet from my auntie's, and my uncle's house was up the hill from us.

During family meals, no one spoke. My sisters, my mother, my father, and I sat together at the table, but no one talked—ever. It was not unusual for a whole week to pass without any of us saying a single word. Though we lived on the farm with my auntie and her family and my uncle and his family, not once did we all get together—*nor any of my extended family*—not even to celebrate a holiday or birthday or special occasion.

So, on top of the Japanese cultural influence of children being silent and *The Way of the Samurai* demeanor, the absence of any conversation in my house deeply impacted the development of my emotions and personality. Looking back to my childhood as an adult, I realized that the lack of connection and communication was rooted in family jealousy and ego and acted out in grudges, disputes, and ongoing fighting.

With no conversation in my family, I had to learn English by playing with my cousins, although they learned to speak Japanese better than I learned English. I also had one American friend who came to play chess occasionally. Learning to speak it was easier than learning to read it, and learning to write it was the most difficult.

Other than playing chess with my friend, I was always outside. I was one of those active, hunter-type of farm kids, armed with my Whammo slingshot, rocks, BB gun, and the bow and arrow I had made. I killed everything that moved—lizards, rabbits, birds. A couple of times, I killed some sparrows and barbecued them, then topped them with soy sauce, and fed them to my cousins. I shot a mockingbird once and tore its flesh out down to its skeleton.

Gophers were rampant on the farm. I rode my bike up and down, setting traps to catch them. When I collected the dead gophers, I took them home and cut off their tails and put them into a jar. Sometimes, I caught scorpions and put them in the jars, but mostly gophers. Then every week, when my uncle and I counted the number of tails in the jars, I got two bits (a quarter) for each tail. You name it, I killed it.

Wayne Dyer used to say that some people never get hurt; nothing happens to them over their entire life. Amazingly, I never got hurt. I never got bitten by the huge buffalo ants, the rattlesnakes, or the ticks. Even though I put myself in harm's way over and over again, I remained unscathed. I don't know if my passion for killing things was the Samurai part of me, but that's the way I grew up. Today, I can't kill anything. I'm the opposite. I have a deep regard for plants and animals and a true desire to care for them.

I'll never know why, but, as stern and controlling as my mom was during my childhood when we moved to the US, she flipped to the other side. She stopped being tough on me and waiting on me hand and foot. When I pushed my pants and underwear down to sit on the toilet and left them there when I got into the shower and after I left the bathroom, she picked them up every time. She never once told me to do anything. My mom picked up after me like a maid. I'm not exaggerating. She never scolded me again, never put me through the pain again, never forced me to do anything again. I don't know whether it was guilt or something else because we never talked about it, but she gave me free rein to do whatever I wanted.

I had a lot of memorable and difficult experiences, but the horrible ones brought contrast to my awareness. Like The Law of Attraction states, with contrast, desire shows up. At the mature age of eight, I learned to always look forward, never back.

The physical traumas of my childhood ended when we moved to the US, but the unspoken emotional ones created scars and patterns beneath the surface that stayed for many years. The restrictions of needing to be silent and tough during my first eight years had molded me to the extent of not knowing how to have a conversation. I had no clue how to socialize. I was unable to communicate my needs and opinions, or even know what they were. I didn't know what to say, or how to say it. I was terrified to be alone with someone because I didn't know how to handle myself. I never went to parties. I never dated. Well, there was one exception when I accepted a girl's invitation to be her Sadie Hawkins Dance date.

With my capacities so limited, subconsciously, the suppression of my expression had forged an ability to channel my energy in nonverbal and non-emotionally ways. My "friendships" developed in the areas I excelled in, academics and athletics. I was the best in my class in math and sciences. I attracted fake "friends" who only wanted me to help them with their homework.

In addition to academics, athletics was my saving grace. I excelled in track, basketball, and tennis. I started playing basketball when I was ten or eleven and was such a natural that kids two years older than me invited me to play with them. That was the boost my self-esteem needed.

So, my outlet for socializing came in the form of sports camaraderie. In a sense, athletics is what gave me contact with people and the ability to express myself. It's really what kept me going. I was finally able to move the energy of the years of muted self-expression and emotion so that it was no longer bottled up inside me. That movement of energy translated into good health. I was never sick.

My mental aptitude was passed down from my mom and my older sister. They had been class Valedictorians of their respective years at Coachella Valley High School, though the accomplishment was bigger for my sister. She could barely speak English and had to get help writing her speech. Articles were written about both my mom and sister in the local newspaper, which inspired and motivated me. Not many people can say that both their mother and sister were class Valedictorians—*and at the same high school.* I was awarded Best Math Student in my senior year of high school, which was also written about in the local newspaper.

Although my dad didn't engage with me, my uncle's brother-in-law took interest in me and worked with me quite a bit. He was the one who provided some of the mentoring and coaching that my dad didn't. During my freshman and sophomore years of high school, he suggested that I use my aptitude in math and science to become an engineer.

The attitudes and accomplishments of my parents had a huge effect on me. It was my mother who inspired me then, but looking back on my adult years, I saw the influence my dad had on me. I understood why he was muted all those years and how brave and responsible his decisions were. Though he had little engagement with me during my life, I have a deep appreciation for him. If not for his allowing me the space to make my own choices and mistakes, I would not have become the man I am today. In fact, if not for his selfless decision to stay on the island during the war, I would not have been born. Neither would my kids.

When I entered college, I moved out of the house, away from my parents and family life, and away from Japanese culture, and I never looked back.

# Chapter 2

# Hands-Off Parenting

*"Prepare the child for the path,*

*not the path for the child."*

Anonymous

Having never dated, gone to parties, or been alone with a girl, I had to design a way to feel comfortable when I was finally ready to start dating in college. So, I wrote notes for myself before each date, kind of like cheat sheets. I listed different topics of discussion that I could bring up, so that I would have something to talk about. It must have worked, because, at twenty-eight, I popped the question, and she said yes.

Living in Irvine, California, we had our first daughter in 1981. We didn't want two kids in college at the same time, so we planned the timing of our second daughter to be born four years later. After she was born, my wife wanted me to get a vasectomy, but I didn't get one. I think that, subconsciously, I wanted to have a son, so I didn't want to cut my future chances. That worked out because he popped out a year and a half later. Like my mom and dad, I had two daughters and one son.

Playing basketball with my kids and coaching them were probably the most positive things I did as a father for them. The bonding between us might otherwise not have happened. But, other than that, like my dad, I was hands-off. When my kids were home, they were mostly with my wife. If I wasn't day trading, I was gone working, golfing, or socializing with friends. There was a period of a couple of years when I was up before dawn every morning and on the phone with one of my client friends day trading. The bedroom my daughters shared was right next to my desk, so they could hear me talking through the wall, which turned out to have an impact on them as adults.

As they were getting older and began going out with friends and on dates, my wife would tell them to be home at eleven thirty, and I would tell them that one thirty was fine. My wife didn't like the conflicting messages, which caused some challenges. But it all worked out.

After my kids had all moved out of the house, the only time they called me was when they wanted money, especially my son. Even though I didn't actively influence him, he decided to work at an accounting firm. After two years, firm work felt too stuffy, so he got his CPA credential and said goodbye to the firm. He had saved enough money to live on for a year and took off to hang out with a friend in New York. After a year, he went to work in Manhattan for a few years and then moved back to Irvine, California, where he currently works for a real estate company.

My eldest daughter earned a degree in accounting and finance and has been working with me at my firm for about fifteen years. My younger daughter got her teaching credential and taught school for eight years until she decided that she didn't like teaching and came to work for me for a couple of years. Then, her on-the-job training and teaching background enabled her to take an administrative position at a non-profit organization, and later at the company where she works now. She also works for me part-time with a couple of our major clients. So, all three of my kids work in my field, with no interference from me.

When I was asked what I want for my kids, I answered that I don't want anything for them. Unlike most parents, I never said, *"I want this for you and that for you,"* and I never will. That would be me telling them what to do. I don't want to do that. Their life choices are theirs to make. I never meddled in my kids' decisions. I never told them what to do, which courses to take, or even whether they should pursue college. They each made their own choices. I was easygoing with them like I am today like I am with anyone. Maybe it was the influence of my upbringing, but my personality is just naturally that way. Hands-off is my style. I don't try to convince or control. I'm not demanding. I don't tell people what they have to do, what they can't do, or what they should do. Every person is responsible for creating his own life. It's not my life; it's not my business. It's theirs.

During this past decade, as a result of the relationships we developed through working together and being in the same industry, my kids and I have grown closer. Our interests have become more similar. Getting closer and having a stronger connection has been a very positive experience for me. But, it came naturally. They got to choose. And I have no regrets.

# Chapter 3

# Day Trading

*"The stock market is a device for transferring money*

*from the impatient to the patient."*

Warren Buffet

Back in 1966, at the age of nineteen, I began trading stocks. The learning curve period was pretty intense for me, researching, learning the basics of how to trade, and hanging out with some of the brokers. Later, during the dot com era between 1998 and 2000, I began to get serious with more trades and larger amounts of money. There were times when I made a hundred and fifty trades in a day. At that point in the bubble, everything was going up and up and up. Here's a funny story about an experience I had.

*My friend and I jumped on an option that brought me four and a half million dollars that same day. I took part of the money and built a swimming pool in the backyard for my kids. Within a year, I lost all of the money in the market, except the money I spent on the pool. I didn't get upset. I wasn't trading for the money. Trading, for me, was playing a game. The funny part is that my kids grew up, and no one was using the pool anymore, so I spent twenty thousand to have it taken out and the hole filled in. The whole experience might have been some kind of metaphor or life lesson; I'm not sure. But we all laugh about that swimming pool.*

Before the bubble burst in the Spring of 2000, I was ahead by six and a half million dollars. When it popped, I had to stop. I had no more money left to trade with, no more money to burn. But again, for me, trading wasn't about money. It was about gambling and trading and playing the game. Of course, losing that much money bothered me, but I wasn't devastated. We laughed about that too.

In 2008, money came in through some real estate transactions I made, and I used that to start trading again. I lost most of it and I stopped again.

My son-in-law became interested in trading through his friends' influence, and then my daughter started dabbling in it with him. She's a little more aggressive than he is, so I lent seed money to her to open her own account to start trading. All of that opened the door to our conversations about trading, which created more of a bond between us. She took off with it and did really well. I was way ahead until some of the stocks started declining, but I had learned my lesson and didn't lose all my money that time.

Over the years, I had been searching for a trading group that would really teach me how to make good money. I spent thousands of dollars on various groups that claimed to be the silver bullet but weren't. In fact, I lost money by following their recommendations. In the Spring of 2021, my daughter introduced me to a truly unique group. I liked their strategies and decided to use them to start trading again, which is when I began doing consistently well. They are changing the whole industry of the financial world, with their educational platform of videos and guidance, trading their own money, and their transparency in showing their profits or losses. I've made good money and am really happy with them, so much so that I told my daughter that she didn't have to pay back the seed money loan. It was my gift to her for introducing me to the group.

Playing options can get a little tricky. Before the market opened last week, I saw the prices on the option I was playing and calculated how much I would win or lose. What I hadn't noticed was that I added one too many zeros in my calculation. I thought that I was going to lose a ton of money when the market opened—a ton meaning *one point five million.*

Instead of panicking or getting mad at myself and all stressed out, I looked at it from a positive viewpoint. *If I lose one point five million dollars, I won't have money to trade anymore, so I'll have to stop trading. With that extra time and not being distracted by the market every day, I'll be able to focus more on other things.*

I keep data sheets to track my trading and position, but I deleted all my data tracking when I got to the office that day, thinking that I wouldn't be trading anymore and wouldn't need it. I was honestly ready and prepared to stop trading permanently. Then, when the market opened and I saw my option, I realized that I had made a mistake in my earlier calculation and that I only lost a hundred and fifty thousand, not one point five million. I was relieved.

Later, I was pleasantly surprised that the position I had on the option ended up turning a profit. So, instead of losing a hundred and fifty thousand, I made sixty thousand.

As I looked back at that morning, I saw that the whole experience was a simulated program that I had unconsciously attracted to myself, and I passed. In my mind, I lost the money, but I didn't lose my center. The experience was an opportunity for me to see how I would respond if I did lose one point five million dollars and had to stop trading *(and cancel the order for my new Tesla, a story that comes in a later chapter)*. I saw how I was able to stay in a high emotional frequency and not be adversely affected by the monetary loss that I thought I had and the decision that I would no longer be trading. My mindset had easily shifted into a positive perspective that would allow me to focus more on my work and other things every day without the distraction of trading. In the end, none of that was true, and I was happy that it wasn't. It was a rollercoaster ride, but, regardless of being down or up, I was okay either way.

Trading has been fun. I'm not making millions anymore, but I'm doing okay. I do it for the experience, the fun, and the adventure. I think it stimulates my dopamine release and the good feeling that results. I used to go to Vegas a lot, which I don't anymore, so this is my simulation outlet and my stimulation outlet—*not that I need more stimulation*. It's funny. I calm down every morning with my meditation and spiritual practices and then jump into day trading and get restimulated. But, that practice and my understanding of the universe are what keep me calm when I trade. If I lose five thousand dollars, it doesn't bother me. I don't get upset or react. My emotions don't go up and down. They're always even, like *The Way of the Samurai*.

# Chapter 4

# Stuck in the Eddy

*"Sometimes, when things are falling apart,*

*they may actually be falling into place."*

Unknown

I began drinking in college, mostly beer and socially at first, and then more frequently as I got older. I drank to lower my inhibitions, so I could communicate more easily and not feel shy. Playing basketball, golfing, and drinking with a core group of friends became my regular routine. I thought my life purpose was drinking, going to bars, hanging out with friends, and having a good time.

During those years, I worked hard during the mornings, beginning around six a.m. I didn't have as many clients back then, so my work was finished around eleven o'clock. There were four different drinking spots that I went to alone and acquainted with the different waitresses. But, it wasn't all for fun. I actually attracted a good client by going to different spots.

When I did meet someone for drinks, we typically met at Hooters around eleven thirty in the morning. My golfing buddies would join us around three or four in the afternoon. If it was on the day of the week that we played basketball, my basketball buddies would come in at that time and drink with us. Then we'd play basketball, which produced a lot of fun and laughter, sliding and falling down on the court. After basketball, we would go out for more drinks. Then, three of us would drive to a Japanese hostess bar in Costa Mesa for more drinks and entertainment. When we got our bill around one or one thirty in the morning, it was often about a thousand dollars.

My extreme passion for playing golf is a positive version of OCD. I used to carry that passion to the extreme. I mean, I was *really* into golf....*and betting on golf.* That's just what we did, golf and bet on golf. And we put a lot of money on the line, so if one of us didn't play well, it meant a loss of three or four hundred dollars. So, I liked to practice—*a lot*—in the mornings before work and on the weekends. One year, I decided to track how many rounds I golfed. I counted two hundred and sixty-five, including the back nine.

A friend had rented a condo for a business trip in Pebble Beach one year and invited me to come up and golf with him. When I told my wife, she told me that I couldn't go. I said okay, but I usually get what I want. So, I left really early in the morning and drove up to Pebble Beach, played two rounds of golf with my friend, drove home, and was at the table in time for dinner. She never knew. I don't accept no for an answer. I find a way.

My friend and I wanted to see how many golf courses we could play in one day. We played eighteen at Sandpiper in Santa Barbara, then drove inland and played another eighteen, and then drove north to Pebble Beach and played seventeen. The only reason we didn't play eighteen was that it had gotten so dark that we couldn't see the course.

During the years that I was drinking a lot, I was pulled over by the police five times for speeding or weaving. One time, I was stopped by two female cops near my home. This was before breath analyzers were used. They took me through all the tests, walking backwards, touching my nose, and holding my arms out. I was in pretty good condition, because of my years running, playing basketball, and competing athletically, so I passed all the tests. One of the cops looked at me afterwards and said, *"Oh you like Kirin beer."* I wondered why she said that, and I told her, *"No, I like Coors Light."* She pointed to my sweatshirt with a big Kirin logo on the front from a tournament I had been in, and she and her partner laughed. They just told me to drive home carefully and let me go.

My ego was so big that it got in my way more often than not. One of my friends had talked about The Landmark Forum that he attended ten years earlier and how much it changed his life. He kept suggesting that I go, but I wasn't interested. What I couldn't see yet was that I wasn't ready. My drinking lifestyle was blocking my vision.

On my birthday in 2008, everything changed. My golfing buddies and I had a tradition of getting together at our watering hole every year to celebrate each other's birthdays. On the day my birthday came around in March, it was raining pretty hard. Only a couple of friends showed up to celebrate with me. I took it personally and got really down and upset. On the way home, I called one of the guys who didn't show up and screamed F-bombs at him for twenty minutes. He stayed on the phone with me and took it all in, but at the end of the call, I told him not to call me or contact me and that I was disconnecting from the whole group. For whatever reason, and without knowing what it all meant, that was the day that I had had enough.

# Chapter 5

# Shedding the Ego
# and Filling the Spiritual Void

*"The difference between who you are and what you want to be*

*is what you do."*

Unknown

Disconnecting with my drinking friends left me with a lot of time on my hands and a big hole in my identity. Around that time, the receptionist at our firm told me that her husband had prostate cancer. Thinking I could help in some way, I wanted to learn about it. For the first time, I got myself a library card and started going to the Irvine Public Library.

Eventually, I ended up noticing different books and topics that interested me and expanded my world. But during that first visit, I was focused on helping her husband. What I didn't know was that this was a synchronistic unfolding. I found a cassette about prostate health and listened to it. The voice of the author resonated with me so much that I ended up buying one of his books. In it, he recommended studying *A Course In Miracles.* I had never heard of it, so I did some research and then ordered the *A Course In Miracles* book on Amazon.

My curiosity was piqued. A few days later, I located a local *A Course In Miracles* group that met regularly at the Unity Church of Tustin. I decided to visit the church to see what it was all about, and it was only five miles from my office. So, one day at lunch, I drove over and saw that the bookstore was open. I walked in and asked the woman there, Ruthann, if she had the *A Course In Miracles* book. I wanted to know what it looked like before it came in the mail. When I got back to the office that day, the Amazon package was sitting on my desk. My book had arrived while I was looking at it in the bookstore. That was the moment I realized that I had received a message. Signs and synchronicities were going to become a part of my life, or they had already been and I wasn't paying attention.

At *A Course In Miracles* book study at the church that Saturday, I met two gentlemen who quickly became my good friends and teachers. They taught me about the course and fast-tracked me on the topic of spirituality, which was a brand-new world for me. I studied intensely and immediately began applying everything I learned in my life. Unconsciously, I was hungry for inner growth and spiritual connection, and I never missed a single Saturday meeting or gathering for the next five and a half years.

A few months into this new stage of my life, I was still looking for things to fill the void the absence of my friends and drinking had left. Out of the blue, I signed up for The Landmark Forum. It was so unplanned that I didn't even tell my friend who had been wanting me to go. It happened just like that, in the moment, which was becoming a new way of living for me. That's when my life changed by one hundred and eighty degrees. The Landmark was amazing. It brought out my buried emotions and really moved me to connect and open my heart and take the actions that I couldn't take before. I reached out to my sister, which I had never done, and we got together and talked, like healthy families do, about life and whatever came up. Landmark opened the door for me to connect with more people in a more authentic and heart-centered way. It also brought me to a place where I could begin to shed my ego.

A friend and I were talking about cars, and I had a Corvette at the time. When I told him that I had a two-seater, he said, *"You know why I don't have a two-seater? Because it limits the number of people you can be with to only two."* That really struck me. The following week, I sold my flashy black convertible Corvette and bought a Dodge Ram SUV. Talk about contrast.

My estrangement from my golfing buddies enabled me to shift out of my excessive drinking lifestyle, which was the best thing I could have done. My kidneys had been hurting from over twenty-five years of heavy drinking. My decision saved my kidneys and my life. There was no occasion to drink like that anymore. I no longer needed that drinking habit to be comfortable in my skin. I have a glass or two of wine when I go out to dinner now and in communion with my friends after our yoga night, but I don't need to have a third and fourth and fifth drink, or drink every day like I used to. I filled the void from not drinking with things that deepened my journey into myself and my spirituality.

My drinking buddies reached out to me after a couple of years, but by then, I had been developing circles of other friends to hang out with. I met up with them, but never connected with them in the same way that we had for all those years because I wasn't the same person. I feel fortunate and grateful for that estrangement. If I hadn't stopped that heavy drinking, I wouldn't be here today. I'd be underground somewhere, probably in Hell.

Speaking of Hell, I used to believe in Heaven and Hell, but I've come to know that idea is part of the ego's fear. EGO is an acronym for Edging God Out. I think God and the Universe just plucked me out of the eddy I had been stuck going around and around in and said, *You've already experienced the other side, the dark side of separateness. Now that you've opened your heart and seen your light, you get to experience the spirit of life.*

I never went to therapy. I don't believe in psychiatry. They always want to go back into the past. Going back to the past to talk about all the circumstances that brought you pain only brings you back to that energy of victimhood and pain again. As long as you talk about it, it keeps you there. That's how The Law of Attraction works—*the energy you focus on, you attract.* Digging up old dirt and focusing your energy on the past facilitates The Law of Attraction bringing your past energies back into your present. Going backwards never works, because you attract what you feel and focus on in every moment. Any unresolved issues I had just worked themselves out as I evolved organically and spiritually

Although *A Course In Miracles* was the first door I opened in my spiritual journey, several key people and teachings have influenced me. The Landmark Forum, Joe Dispenza, Bruce Lipton, Joe Vitale, Eckhart Tolle, and Wayne Dyer are a few. The most impactful have been Esther Hicks, The Law of Attraction, and Sonja Grace. As I absorbed each of their teachings, I evolved to a place that allowed me to find my voice.

# Chapter 6

# Finding My Voice

*"It's not about finding your voice.*

*It's about giving yourself permission to use your voice."*

Kris Carr

Psychologists have said that the first six years of your life form ninety per cent of your personality. They say that you're pretty impressionable during those first six years, and after that, your personality and behavior are set in stone. I don't believe any of that. People can change. People are malleable. It all depends on what you choose to believe. Belief is what creates your reality.

By 2011, my accounting firm had been growing by word of mouth, but slowly. I asked my nephew, who was working with me at the time if he thought that I should do some networking to bring in more clients. He thought that was a good idea, and he encouraged me. So, there I was, a virgin in connecting with people, and I thought, *Ok, now what do I do?* I had never learned even the basics of a simple conversation, let alone networking in a big group of people one after the other. I didn't know the first thing about how to give a presentation. Even though I had begun my spiritual journey, I was still muted and rarely spoke.

I took one of the biggest leaps of my life and joined Toastmasters. After a year and a half of practicing how to speak in front of the group, I was finally ready to begin networking and presenting, and I joined BNI (Business Networking International). From there, I joined the Holistic Chamber of Commerce, which introduced me to a holistic mastermind group. Then, I began attending assorted networking events, some of which I joined, like the Inside Edge, Provisor, The Irvine Chamber of Commerce, and Wake Up OC. Through this chain of networking connections, I began meeting people who became valuable key relationships that supported and collaborated with me in my business, my investments, my health, and in the writing of this book.

Before 2011, I hadn't wanted to speak to people or socialize. Toastmasters and BNI opened me up completely. Once that channel of communication was unblocked, I began to feel comfortable in my skin, which enabled me to be more comfortable with people one on one. I learned how to be more at ease in conversations, doing presentations, and networking, all of which translated into my growing the firm at a faster rate. It expanded my interests and knowledge about life and about people. I was no longer that shy, muted person and began looking forward to getting to know people now, doing things together, and developing collaborative relationships to create a bigger picture. I'm a different person today, in part, because of those organizations. If I hadn't asked my nephew about networking, and if he hadn't encouraged me, none of these would have happened.

If you have the belief that, because your uncle had cancer and your aunt had cancer, then it's in your genes and you're going to get cancer, *then you will get cancer—because that's what you believe*. If you believe that your family is fat, so your fat, and that's ok, because you can't help it and there's nothing you can do about it, *then you'll stay fat*. A lot of people come from that place of believing that their health, marriage, happiness, finances, or future is out of their control, or that their destiny is predetermined by external factors. It's sad and unfortunate that people put those kinds of limiting, fear-based beliefs out there because they convince other people to believe them too.

Whom we become is not about our DNA. Epigenetics has proven that genes can change. It's also not about being destined to carry forward the negative or dysfunctional behaviors from our youth. If that were true, I would still be horribly shy and awkward, unable to hold a conversation, constantly afraid to do something the wrong way, and afraid to try new things. There is so much proof that these limiting assumptions are simply not true. I am proof. I've proven that people can make great changes. I broke the habit of going to bars and drinking every day. I broke the belief that I couldn't have easy, fulfilling conversations. I found my voice. I learned to speak.

# Chapter 7

## The Gifts of My Experience

## Silence, Resiliency, Boundaries, Compassion, Generosity

*"Strength doesn't come from what you can do.*

*It comes from overcoming the things you once thought you couldn't."*

Rikki Rogers

**Silence**

Although I learned to speak, the silence I had grown up in taught me a lot. Even prior to discovering my lineage, I was like the emotionless Samurai. The silence, and what my parents each modeled for me in different ways, taught me to find my own inner strength and tap into it, without knowing I was doing it.

When I was going to school in Los Angeles at nineteen and twenty, my transportation was my Honda s90 motorcycle. I often rode to my sister's house in the San Fernando Valley area, taking my bike on Sepulveda Boulevard up the hill and then down into the valley. One day, on my way to visit, I was riding downhill at seventy-five or eighty miles an hour, when a car suddenly appeared in front of me. I had to brake fast, and I flipped and rolled, watching the sparks from my bike as it rolled down the hill without me. When my body finally came to a stop and I got up, the driver, who had pulled over, started screaming at me. *"It was your fault! You're going too fast!"* I said, *"Don't worry about it; just go."* She left.

I had some bruises and a little blood, but nothing serious. I walked to the middle of the road to pick up my helmet, but another car came and ran over it and dragged it down the hill. I walked to the bottom of the hill to get my bike, picked it up, and walked it to the service station. The guy whose car had dragged my helmet handed my dented helmet to me. I asked the service station attendant for one of their rubber mallets, and I pounded out the dents as well as I could. I put the helmet on my head, got back on my bike, and rode to my sister's. We ate dinner, pretty much in silence, and I rode my bike home. I never said a word to her about what had happened. To this day, I haven't told her. It's never been my style. There's no need to drum it all up again just to tell someone about it. That just creates drama and unnecessary emotion. What was done was done. I didn't need anyone to make a fuss over me. I'm the same today. I don't need drama.

Like I learned at eight years old, you can only go forward. In the present, I stay calm. My emotions don't go up and down much. If I lose fifty thousand dollars in the stock market, it might bother me, but I don't get crazy over it. I just let it go. My attitude is, *so what; I'll make it up tomorrow.* I don't get stressed. Part of that is because I was raised to be silent through all the painful experiences and mute my feelings. But, part is also knowing that talking and dramatizing everything that happens to people doesn't help anyone. It only keeps the story going.

**Compassion and Generosity**

I've always had a heart for people, a deep compassion. I get a strong sense of satisfaction in helping others, especially people who are down and out. During my freshman year of college, I was at the bank, standing in line behind a man who was having trouble cashing his out-of-state check. I stepped up and offered to give him cash for it if he wrote a check to me. He did. Unfortunately, his check bounced. But it didn't bother me.

In a similar situation in the parking lot of my office, a guy was in a dire circumstance and needed money, so I offered him some cash if he wrote me a check. He did, and his check bounced. But it was no big deal. I helped him because it felt good to help, not because I wanted something for it, or I wanted to see if he was good at it. It wasn't to prove anything.

I have done a lot of stupid things in my life, though. Most were simple things, like giving a hundred-dollar tip to a nice waitress at lunch or dinner. I'm sure that in my younger years, some of my actions were subconsciously motivated by my ego or grandstanding. I wanted to be liked, or recognized, or tell a unique story that people wanted to hear. If I mentioned all the different things I've done, people would think I was nuts.

One Friday night during my heavy drinking years, a new bar waitress waited on me. She was nice, so I told her that I was going to give her my credit card to use over the weekend. My friends all looked at me and said, *"Sam, what are you doing?"* I replied, *"Let's just see what she does."* I monitored the card over the weekend, to be ready to take action if I needed to. By the end of the weekend, she had charged fifteen hundred dollars, and she gave me my credit card back on Monday. That was me grandstanding. You can ask a million people if anyone would do what I did, and maybe one person would. That was a unique story that I could tell and people would want to listen.

But seriously, giving money to a stranger feels good to me. It's part of my personality, a combination of fearlessness and compassion. When I go to Vegas and play blackjack, I tip the dealer. Sometimes, I bet money for the dealer instead of tipping, and I give her the money if the bet wins. One time, I bet ten dollars for myself and twenty-five dollars for the dealer. She lost, and I started laughing, *"You lost more money than I did!"*

Besides wanting to help people by giving them money, the crazy things I do with money also come from my viewpoint on money. I've never had the perspective that most people do, which is to worship money as if it were a god. Most people make it the highest goal and focus on what they can do to make money, or what they can do to make someone participate in something so that they can make more money. To them, everything is about money, money, money. They're so afraid of losing control or being fooled or taken advantage of by someone who sold them a bad bill of goods or giving money to someone who might take the money and run that they never take the risk of giving the money. Or, if they did once, but lost, they became terrified or bitter and swore never to do it again.

To me, money is just a tool. I've always had compassion for helping people, and money seems to be the most valuable way for people to receive help. I've never worried about money. I'm not attached to it. Even if someone's check bounced, I would give them cash again. The lack of payback doesn't teach me not to do it again, because it's just money. I've made millions and lost millions. Losing money doesn't bother me. With that attitude and energy, the universe always gives back to me.

Years and years ago, a couple was referred to me for accounting services. I felt their need for an honest, competent accountant, so I opened a heart-to-heart connection with them. From that space, I never charged them during the twenty years of doing their accounting, and we became good friends. Consequently, the husband, who was a gynaecologist, provided his services to a couple of my friends at no charge. They were so grateful for my referral. Compassion pays itself forward. It always comes back to you.

Over the years, I've taken on clients who were trying to recover from a difficult past. If people are struggling, I do their taxes at no charge. And I'm okay with that because they were in a bad situation. For a few, I've continued waiving my fee for thirty-plus years. For me, it's not about the money. It's about helping people.

Money is something I've always enjoyed working and playing with. I manage several investment portfolios, including those of my nephew and a couple of my employees. When I initially approach people to offer my expertise, I explain to them that investing money in CDs earns less than two per cent, whereas other types of investments have no limit, and if I manage their money, they risk nothing. If my investment choice creates a loss, I make up for it in some way and recoup their money for them. And they're not committed to a time period; I invite them to just say the word if they want to get out. Once a week, I go over the numbers with them and share with them the actions I took and why. Their risk is zero, and their upside is limitless.

I don't ask for anything in exchange, but if someone wants to compensate me for helping them, because something I've done has been beneficial to them, I just tell them to donate to my nonprofit. I don't need the money. I help them because I'm good at what I do, and I get satisfaction and fun from it. Helping and educating people brings me joy.

## Boundaries

I help when I want to help, but I don't let people walk on me. Some are takers, always taking what they can from others. I give those kinds of people a very loose rope and a lot of room. It's up to them to decide whether to tie the rope around their own necks. Some don't know when to stop and end up taking too much advantage. I don't have to do much; they hang themselves. I have boundaries, but they're wide, and I put my foot down when they've been crossed. Sometimes when that happens, I just part ways. At some future point, they may realize that they should have done something for me. Maybe they should have treated me to lunch. Maybe they should have given me a gift. Maybe they should have given me some amount of payment, or done a favor for me. But I don't expect that. Some are takers who are always taking. I'm always a giver until I'm taken advantage of.

One of my clients introduced me to a well-known, highly revered health practitioner who had made tons of money helping people through his books and teachings. At the height of his success, he was a guest on Oprah's show. But, after years and years of healing thousands of people all over the world, one of his customers filed a complaint. As a result, he was prosecuted and imprisoned for a year and a half. By the time I met him, he lost everything and was in serious trouble.

I spent hours and hours unraveling everything for him, talking with the IRS, finding all the liability releases, and cleaning up all the mess that he was in. During the five years that I helped him, he never offered to pay me, and I never asked to be paid. After I cleaned up his mess, I continued to help him for a while. He mentioned a few times that he had a special pendant that he wanted to give me for all the services I provided. But, he never brought it. One day, he called to ask me to provide a consultation for his girlfriend who needed help. At the end of the consultation, he told me that he forgot again to bring the pendant and would mail it to me when he got home.

A couple of months passed, and the pendant never came. He called to ask me to do some more work for him, because the IRS was asking questions. That's the day I put my foot down. I told him that I didn't want to ever hear about him or see him again, and I said goodbye. I released him. The pendant arrived shortly afterwards.

Another client had a health food restaurant in Irvine that I happened to find. He was struggling, so I helped him with all of his bookkeeping, accounting, tax returns, and payroll over the next ten years. He often called me and invited me to his restaurant and treated me to dinner or lunch, but he was always hanging around my table asking questions about one thing or another, constantly picking my brain, and probing me for information.

At the time, I was doing real estate syndications, and he invested in one of my projects in Michigan. Three months after investing, he came to me and asked if he could get his investment money back. When I told him that I would see if I could find someone to take his position, his tone changed. He became really forceful and told me, *"I want it NOW. And if you don't get it to me by this Friday, I'm going to sue you."*

On April 1st, two weeks before the tax deadline, he came to my office and asked if I could do his tax return, as I had done for ten years. I told him, *"No, I'm done with you. I can't do your taxes anymore."* He didn't really say anything. He knew that he deserved that. Soon after that, he made a fifty per cent return on his real estate investment, which made him so happy that he changed his mind about wanting his money back. He's still in the real estate syndication today. He made a lot of money from my help and advice. About a year later, he called and asked if we could get together for lunch. I told him no. I never heard from him again.

When enough is enough, I put my foot down. I not only stop helping; I also cut ties. And every time I do, something positive comes from it. During the years I was helping the health practitioner, he introduced me to his son, who later became my partner in co-creating a unique, one of its kind, sound-healing wine glass. They are handmade glasses that resonate with a beautiful sound for about forty-five seconds. The sound improves the aroma and the taste of the wine and exponentially raises the vibrational experience for wine drinkers. It's the only one in the world.

### Resiliency

A friend and I used to go deep-sea fishing off the Catalina and Santa Barbara Islands. I had just finished reading a book that motivated me so much, I became a vegan. My friend and I had already bought tickets for the trip, but at the last minute, I didn't want to go. I didn't want to eat fish. I didn't even want to fish for fish. I told my friend, but he talked me into coming anyway, just not fishing. I agreed, but with some resistance. During that fishing trip, we experienced the strongest winds we'd ever had. The waves rocked the boat so forcefully that everyone was vomiting. No one could fish. In the midst of it, my friend looked at me and said, *"You're powerful! You made it so that no one else could fish either!"*

I think that part of my resilient attitude comes from the pain I experienced as a child before moving to the US, and the terrible shyness I struggled with through school and college. Those influences and my ancestral Bushido way have really directed me into the man I am today. My style and the way I treat people reflect that of the honorable Samurai.

People think that you need to heal your past, but saying that you need to heal yourself is actually a self-defeating statement. It means that you believe something is wrong or damaged or bad about you. Even just saying that you need to heal your past will keep you back. The energy in those beliefs, and the words that express them, is that powerful. In my opinion, there's really no such thing as healing yourself.

The only way to evolve is to look forward and connect to feeling good. You've gotten here because of all you experienced and learned and integrated from your past. I understand all of this now. I'm in great appreciation for all of the experiences of my past, but I would never want to go back to redo it because what happened there brought me here.

The muting of my youth actually served me. The cultural and environmental influence of my ancestry and upbringing helped shape the positive aspects I exhibit today. It's a choice you make to take what you were given, learn the value in it, and use it to make yourself stronger, wiser, more compassionate, and better for it.

# Chapter 8

# Pioneering A Holistic Identity

*"The first step toward getting somewhere*

*is to decide you're not going to stay where you are."*

JP Morgan

As I continued my journey of spirituality and self-discovery, I began really liking myself and valuing what I was becoming. Understanding the miracles of the universe and how life works and knowing that we are always loved and guided allowed me to begin to see the Divinity in me in a way that I had never seen or known before. All of this naturally led me to want to take better care of myself and my body.

I'd always been active in sports, but I had been feeling a need for an extra edge. In the beginning, it came from a somewhat egoic desire to enhance my physical appearance and look younger. Later, it evolved into a desire to be healthier and more vital, to ensure my ability to live a long, optimal life, and thrive.

One of my investment collaborations is with a client who is a biochemist. He had developed and patented a cellular activating formulation of the antioxidant, glutathione, and I wanted to support him, so we created a nutraceutical company and began manufacturing the glutathione in pill form. In the beginning, we tried to sell it in the traditional methods, but we couldn't make headway. So, we merged with a multi-level marketing company that had been selling an inferior glutathione NAC product. Our product is three hundred per cent more bioavailable than NAC, and it doesn't have a sulfur smell. It's also scientifically based, so it's well-accepted in the scientific community. It's done so well that it's now available in over seventeen countries.

When I joined The Holistic Chamber of Commerce in 2013, I was introduced to a whole new group of people who were into holistic lifestyles and natural health solutions. As I began learning about some of them, my knowledge of natural health and anti-aging grew, and I tried more and more different products and practices. It eventually developed into a health regime. Although I didn't start getting healthy until after I turned sixty-five, I've changed quite a lot of my former habits. My prior golfing OCD transmuted into my extreme passion and practice of spirituality, health, meditation, and yoga.

I've tried a lot of things, dropped some, started others, and am continually meeting new people with new health products, practices, or services. Many of them are from networking events I attend, like the person who developed a mat called Vibrate that stimulates the brain with different frequencies of music. In 2021, I added eight new practices and products. Some of my current products and practices include: CVAC machine; Bemer; hyperbaric chamber; Asea cellular water; aragonite; the Avacen machine; supplements; meditation; yoga; hiking; listening to spiritual mentors; using my energy wine glass product; Kangen water; and a telomeres product. I also listen to Dr Joe Dispenza and practice his mind methods to change the direction of my health, emotions, and consciousness. I try lots of things to see what works and what doesn't work. None of it hurts, and all of it helps. All of it contributes.

The one area of health I don't have that most people would consider healthy choices is food. I have no dietary restrictions, allergies, limitations, or observances. I did go vegan for a while (during that deep sea fishing trip) after reading *The Greening of America,* a book about the cruelty to animals used for human food consumption. After reading that, I couldn't eat meat or seafood anymore. But that only lasted for about three months. I eat anything—chocolate, dessert, sugar, red meat, and seafood.

One of the aspects of health I'm best at is staying centered. I don't worry about things. Worry causes stress, and stress brings adverse health conditions. Like everyone, I have opportunities to get stressed, but I don't let them come in. So, I have no stress. At the age of seventy-five, my hair is still black. I just keep going. I must be doing something right.

My journey of personal health eventually became intertwined with my work. About ten years ago, my BNI chapter president gave a ten-minute pep talk, encouraging us to really make our presentations interesting. It struck me when he said, *"Don't be like an accountant, talking about tax law changes or taxes."* I thought, *I am an accountant. What am I going to talk about? I do taxes, so I need to talk about taxes.*

I had been talking to people for a while about The Law of Attraction being the main focus, I use in running my business. It's a way of allowing, not controlling. This holistic aspect of my personality influences my management of the people in my accounting firm, just like it did my parenting style and—I manage them by not managing them. Whereas most CPA firms operate with a lot of control, I have never asked my staff to work overtime. I don't have to ask them to get caught up by working more. They just do.

When I use the term holistic, I mean things relating to natural health and spiritual health. I also mean viewing the whole of something to improve it, rather than viewing the parts separately, whether it's a business, body, relationship, money, nature, or a problem to be remedied. I don't only use holistic resources for my health and work. I live a holistic lifestyle all the way around.

As I reflected on this parallel between my organic work and parenting styles, it occurred to me that I had not only become holistic in my personal life, but also in my work. I was not a typical accountant; I was a holistic accountant. In addition to managing my firm holistically, I had increasingly found myself providing holistic health guidance to my clients, sharing with them what I learned and incorporating it into my personal health, as far as holistic practices or products to help their personal conditions or situations. My perspective is that when you feel well, you do well—in your personal life, your relationships, your work, and your purpose.

With that observation, I thought, why not brand my uniqueness and promote myself as a holistic accountant? I acted on that inspiration immediately and paid five thousand to one of the BNI members to help me brand my new identity with business cards, brochures, and other things I needed. I was ready to officially take on my new role as The Holistic Accountant.

People frequently ask me what a holistic accountant is, and I explain it like this. Accountants are like rear-view mirrors, always looking behind at what's been done. For example, when their clients need a financial statement for a bank or creditor's request, the accountants go back to the past and crunch the numbers and create a statement. After the client submits it to the bank or creditor, the client does nothing with the statement, because it serves no purpose to him. However, as a holistic accountant, I'm forward-looking, creating possibilities for the future of my clients.

Most companies spend their advertising budget externally, rather than work internally. The problem this generates always lies with the CEO and the owner of the company, where the big ego resides. They're always afraid to lose control of the company, so they focus on being able to control the people, which makes them feel good about themselves. They tell the people what to do, and the people do it. It's a power grab that creates fear in the staff. Most people work from a foundation of fear—fear of getting fired, or fear of making a mistake and getting reprimanded or fired because of it. When a company creates an environment with a lot of fear, the creativity of the staff is suppressed and collapses.

The loss of creativity actually starts at the top, with the fear of losing control. Most companies create an agenda, and they discuss what's on the agenda logically, one step at a time. This method closes off all kinds of possibilities that could show up, other things that could be more creative and more meaningful and expand the production of the employees and the livelihood of the company.

Traditionally, the CEO simply fires a person who's not happy, not creative, not productive, or not following the rules. The logic they use in firing someone is, in not having to pay that salary, the company will save fifty thousand dollars a year and increase the bottom line. However, they neglect to look at the wider and long-term view. They'd save so much more money by decreasing the turnover and increasing creativity if they work with the people in the company and create a fearless work environment that cultivates a culture that employees thrive.

If you give a person enough responsibility, they take it upon themselves to finish it. And if you are compassionate and show them that you care about them, it just all works without effort or stress or time waste. If CEOs let their company run organically, employees will leave naturally, of their own accord, via the law of attraction operating in their lives and in the company. The company heads won't have to spend so much time and energy on firing and hiring and training and administrative responsibilities. Everything works organically.

My concept is that, if you build the people, the people will build the company. Companies need to create a climate in which people can make their own decisions, individually or collectively, not from an agenda. When you work with people and create an environment filled with appreciation, communication, and no fear, no one worries when someone makes a mistake. By creating an environment with less fear, creativity soars, possibilities open, and the company grows organically and successfully. It becomes a happier place to work where everyone gets along. As a result, employee absenteeism decreases and retention increases, because employees want to be there. All of this doesn't happen immediately, but it happens.

Holistic Management Guidance is something I'm passionate about, but not for the purpose of attracting more clients. I have enough clients. I'm interested in offering this to companies who are open to making their company heads and their businesses more sustainable. If they embrace my suggestions and implement them, my fee is based on the benefit they receive from applying the guidance.

My purpose is not to take away the company accountant's job, but to share my ideas with the company accountants, work with them, and bring them to a different point of view. Accountants are difficult to work with. They're very close-minded and don't have relationship or interpersonal skills. They don't think they need them, because they just sit quietly behind a desk, crunching the numbers, and giving the company what it wants. I can identify with this because that's whom I used to be, a person without relationship and interpersonal skills. That's what drew me to accounting in the first place—*that and the desire not to be killed in a chemist's lab*. But I have them now, which is one of the ways I'm especially equipped to help accountants grow their skills and grow the company.

When you build the people, the people build the company. Yes, I do taxes and ledgers and books, but as a holistic accountant, I operate a few layers larger than that. Here's an example of how that works for the benefit of all. One of my employees had been working with me for about sixteen years, beginning when I had my real estate mortgage company and continuing with me into my accounting business. She was my go-to person for everything, so we had a lot of communication, and I knew her pretty well. I noticed one day that she was irritable and unhappy with the work that she was doing. She didn't say anything to me, but I knew something was bothering her, and I knew it wasn't at the level of her awareness that she could directly access yet.

So, I asked her if she might be interested in taking the four-day Landmark Forum. I told her that I'd take care of the cost and arrangements, and she agreed to do it. Within a week of completing it, she came to me and told me that she needed to leave the firm. Because I had always been so nice to her and took care of her and had a compassionate, hands-off management style, she hadn't wanted to tell me before. The experience of taking the intensive transformational Landmark forum gave her the insight to see her truth and the courage to speak it. When she told me, I didn't complain or get sad or upset. I just told her that I was glad she had realized what she needed to do and that I was fine with her decision. I supported her and told her not to feel bad.

The very next day, my nephew came to the office. He'd never been to the office before or even known where it was. The firm he worked at had a client in the complex near my office, so as he was leaving there, he happened to see my name on our office door. He poked his head in to ask if I had time to talk. I told the client I was working with that I needed to leave for a few minutes, and I stepped out to talk with my nephew. He told me that he had been working too many hours and was thinking about leaving public accounting to go into private accounting. I told him that my long-term employee had just given notice and that her position was open if he'd like to work for me. He said he would. The following week, he told his firm that he had to quit and ended up starting with me in time to work with my employee to learn what she did before she left the firm.

Around that same time, another staff member told me that she wanted to leave. She had left my firm a couple of years earlier.

Before she left, told me not to talk her out of it (because I was so nice that she would feel compelled to stay). I didn't talk her out of it. I wished her well, but she ended up coming back, of her own accord. She handled our more difficult audit clients and wanted to leave because she was overwhelmed by the lack of background experience she felt she needed for the more complex client audits. Even though she had taken courses, she was uncomfortable with her ability and had been putting more and more judgment and pressure on herself. I wanted to help her, but I hadn't been trained in audit accounting. My nephew, on the other hand, had been doing audit accounting at the firm he had just left and knew what he was doing. He came on board with us just in time to take over some of her work. His assistance took the pressure off of her, and she ended up staying with my firm. My nephew became my partner in 2018, and he's still with me today.

The unexpected bonus of this story is, with my nephew's arrival, I was able to retain one of my biggest clients whose business brought in close to fifty per cent of our revenue. That client is still with me today, and so is my audit staff member. She and my nephew saved my firm.

In my holistic style of managing my staff by not managing them and allowing my firm to operate organically with The Law of Attraction, everything always works out. The satisfaction of all involved and the success of my firm are the results of that and the compassionate decision I made to reach out to help my staff member align with herself, by offering her The Landmark Forum.

It doesn't matter where you start your lifestyle change, as long as you start somewhere and keep adding other aspects. Some people start with healthy foods or products. Some start with physical exercises. Some start with spirituality like I did. Others start with meditative mental clearing or emotional heart-opening. One health component improves the whole, which is the meaning of holistic. The formula of all that you do combines together like a complete cocktail.

My yogi had clients come for his medical yoga therapy, hoping to get rid of their neck and shoulder pain. After two or three months, their pain went away and they stopped doing yoga. What they don't understand is that yoga therapy works on all of the mind, body, and spirit. They were just looking for a fix to a circumstance, instead of incorporating yoga into the lifestyle practice, not knowing that it was also improving their mental and emotional health. Without continuing the practice, no matter what it is, you only have a temporary mind fix or relief, and your body's going to break down again.

A lot of people don't understand the value of taking the extra mile. If they knew what it could do for them, they would, but most people don't see the complete picture of how improving their health improves their life. It also creates a positive shift in their business. As their vibration rises, they start attracting different people, because they start calibrating to a different level. They're usually not doing it on purpose; it just happens as a byproduct of all the health changes they make. Things just start showing up, and their whole life changes.

After I got to a certain point of improving my healthy habits, everything just accelerated. My health, my mental clarity, and my vibration all improved, which attracted new things and opportunities and people, like Sonja Grace. We've become pretty good friends now. She'll be coming to LA and I'm going to take her and her husband to a Japanese restaurant. I always tell people not to be in awe of celebrities or worship them, because they're just like everyone else. When I think about the experience of becoming friends with an internationally known person and having dinner with her, I see that it's part of everything that is happening to me.

All the little things I do add up to who I am now. If I took even one part out of the equation of my holistic lifestyle, my whole being shifts. I might still be able to get where I want to be in life without that one thing, but it would take longer and be more difficult and cause more stress and conditions. That's what holistic means. You look at the whole thing and serve the whole. If you drop even one thing that's helping the whole of you to vibrate higher, then the whole of you will vibrate lower.

All parts of life merge into a holistic whole.

# Chapter 9

## Saying Yes ~

## Curiosity, Connection, Causes

*"Always say 'yes' to the present moment.*

*Say 'YES" to it,*

*and see how life suddenly starts working for you,*

*rather than against you."*

Eckart Tolle

As I continued to evolve in my health and spirituality, I felt an increasing desire to support and uplift the spirit of humanity. A lot of my friends were stuck in limited viewpoints, spinning around in their own eddies, and I wanted to see if I could spread the understanding and energy awareness that I had, to help them come out of their unhappiness. But, most of my long-time friends didn't want to come out. With their good time drinking and golfing habits, they didn't want to know what they didn't know. A couple of them actually said to me, *"I don't want to know what you're doing."* They didn't want me to ruin their mindless fun or make them feel guilty for disconnecting from God, Source, or Higher Self. Obviously, I knew that I couldn't help everyone, but if I could get one or two per cent to see the light and make a shift, my effort would be worth it.

I was compelled to play some kind of role in helping others come out of whatever funks they were in and move forward in their lives. Ideas came to help group projects and networks of different people who would enjoy getting together to communicate their dreams and goals. All of these would allow me to be surrounded by the kind of people I wanted to have relationships with.

Humanitarian yearnings inspired ideas of what I could develop. One, in particular, was to manifest and promote some of my visions to large groups of people within the platform of nonprofits. I knew that nonprofits were a successful way to attract people to come on board, collaborate, contribute, and benefit from the specific purpose. My ideas weren't coming from a place of calculated strategy or desire for money. It wasn't about creating for-profit organizations or business ventures. I do things by the seat of my pants. It was about feeling good inside and fulfilling my desire to uplift humanity.

From time to time, I noticed that college students would come to me or call me for advice on career and college. I saw how different the times were, compared to when I was their age, with so many more people and so much competition. They didn't have enough guidance to help them discern the important things they needed to consider and do. It struck me that they needed mentoring. I wanted to find a way to mentor them, but I was just one person. I was talking about it with a friend and said, *"If I could just plant a seed..."*

With those words, the seed for my first nonprofit sprouted. In 2011, I invited the Course In Miracles facilitator and seven friends from the study group to dine with me at a Japanese restaurant. I posed the gathering as an opportunity to get together for a common purpose, for transformation, and for each of them to be a part of a bigger cause. I didn't go into a lot of detail, just enough to determine their level of interest.

Looking back on it now, I think that I was trying to test my voice, to see how well I could express myself and be listened to and understood. It was also a way that I could form connections and relationships. Excited after the dinner gathering, I moved forward and set up a corporation for the nonprofit. I called it Transformation.

Unfortunately, when I followed up with my friends, none seemed interested. They just laughed and questioned my logic. In truth, they just didn't share my higher mindset. With no one on board to resonate with my vision and passion, I canceled the corporation. And I didn't think about it again…

Until I discovered that one of the members of our BNI chapter was a consultant for nonprofits. As soon as I heard her, I made a beeline toward her and scheduled a one-on-one meeting to share my vision. The outcome of that meeting gave me a huge boost of confidence and the support and courage I needed to share it with other members of my chapter. From that, eight members expressed interest. And in 2013, those eight became the founding board members of my first nonprofit, a mentoring organization called, Plant A Seed Institute.

Eight mentors grew to thirteen men and women focused on mentoring millennials, primarily along the career path, which was where we saw the need. We observed that millennials, in general, had a higher education, but they didn't learn communication skills. So, each of the mentors focused on a different area, based on their expertise and passion. My focus was on areas critical for creating successful career paths, like helping them differentiate themselves from others, teaching them to show up, and guiding them to improve their interpersonal communication skills. Within those areas, I stressed the importance of having good energy, attentiveness, presence, high energy, and a smile, among other things. In mentoring them, some of the questions I asked them were, *"How do you show up? How do you separate yourself from the other hundred or more college students who also got straight A's? Why would a company choose you, when you're all identical in your education? How are you going to go higher up the corporate ladder? How are you going to distinguish yourself?"* and *"How do you communicate with people?"*

My desire to connect with people, create relationships, and strengthen communication came from not my lack of friends in the first two decades of life, as well as growing up in a house where no one talked. It also came from having a mother who was at first commanding, and later servant-like and a father who was muted and mostly absent. I had minimal communication and relationships and no one to mentor me in college, jobs, and career beginnings. With the exception of my uncle's brother-in-law and a couple of suggestions from friends in college, I was left on my own to experiment and flounder my way. I felt compassion for others who didn't have anyone and wanted to give them what I needed.

Working with Toastmasters and The Law of Attraction was the catalyst that seeded "Plant A Seed Institute," and BNI was the soil from which it sprouted. As I watched my ideas and connections continue to develop, I became more curious about what other things I could learn, what I could create and contribute, and what else was possible for me in life.

One aspect of my personality is the part that says yes—to *almost everything.* I don't say, *"Well let me think about it."* In my experience, it's gone by the time you think about it. If you don't reach out for that hundred-dollar bill floating in front of you, it'll blow away, or someone else will reach for it. So, I grab it.

Sometimes, saying yes hurts me, but that doesn't stop me from saying yes. If it doesn't work out, it doesn't work out—*so what.* I'm not concerned with wondering if it'll turn out, or worrying if I could get burned. I've been burned many times by people taking advantage of me, but that doesn't stop me from saying yes to the next thing. You can't let fear dictate your possible future.

Look around. Everything and everyone who found you resulted in something positive down the line, even if it's decades later. Those people and circumstances were all there *for you,* to *guide* you in a different direction. That's why it never bothers me that I helped people who ended up turning on me. I just let them go. Certain things stick, and certain things don't. Enough of them stick to create a wider base for me. I'm always supported and taken care of. I never doubt that.

By saying yes and opening myself to opportunities, I've attracted and connected with a wide variety of people. Some have something to contribute to me, or to my desires and dreams. One who comes to mind is the co-creator of Wake-Up OC. Another is his father, an eighty-two-year young retired engineer for the inventor of Whammo. When I met him and his significant other of twenty-five years, we shared some stories and connected on a similar spiritual path. He's open-minded and very bright. He used to be very active but lost his passion for life. He doesn't really do anything anymore, other than eat and drink and watch television with his partner.

I thought it might inspire him and bring some life back into him if he were involved in a humanitarian mission. So, I shared my 100-Year Tour plan with him *(more on this in a later chapter).* He'll turn a hundred years old before I do. When I asked him if he would be interested in being the first person to do the tour, he didn't jump up and say yes, but he was interested. I think that his life force is so low, that he doesn't get excited about anything anymore. He's got some health challenges, like excess weight, hip problems, and lung issues. He carries an oxygen tank.

Being on a holistic and spiritual path, I felt inspired to help him improve his health. So, I asked him if he was open to doing yoga, and if so, I would arrange it for him at no cost to him. The only thing he would need to do is come to the yoga studio in Tustin. When he said that he would, I reached out to my Yogi, to have him work with him a bit and see if he can start feeling better and more comfortable in his body. I also gave him a stem cell patch to determine whether it relieves his hip pain. My plan is to slowly bring him back up to the point where he regains his balance and can walk with no pain and does not carry his oxygen tank. All of these things will reduce his struggle with weight. I have a lot of other modalities that I want to share with him later, but we're trying these two first to see how it goes and if any other issues arise. I think he still feels young, despite his body conditions, and he seems to want to change his health. Regardless of how many or how effective, these resources will enable him to become active again, even if it takes a while. Movement alone will increase his energy and give him new life. And that renewed power and vitality will enable him to generate income from his passion, creative mind, and talent.

Some of the people and offerings I say yes to end up being valuable, and some not. Ultimately, however, they lead me to meet other people who come into my life. That's why I get involved in an assortment of activities. I'm in that space now, where each person I've met, worked with or contributed to, connected me in a positive way to another person or another connection.

Because I say yes to everything—and because I'm always curious—I've developed a diversity of interests, including investing, trading, accounting, insurance, spirituality, crypto-currency, real estate, health, nonprofits, startups, and entrepreneurship. One of the greatest outcomes of this is that I've become more creative and proficient at many things. I'm someone whom others can come to for information on pretty much anything they're considering or wanting to learn about, in a range I call, *from the cradle to the grave*. I'm not a professional in all of these areas, but I've experienced and worked with them. I can also direct people in The Law of Attraction, networking, mentoring, life purpose alignment, and futures market for currency, cattle, wheat, etc.
The world has dozens of individual or specialist advisors, but not one person with the quantity and diversity of first-hand experience. There isn't one thing I haven't personally tried,

learned, or worked with. Rather than talking to a handful or more people to find guidance and recommendations in more than one area of life, people can get multiple perspectives for their developing interests from one person, one-stop.

With that said, I don't share my knowledge and capacities with everybody. Coming from a muted background, I've gotten used to being in the background. I don't blow myself up, which also makes me unique. A person could brag to a group of people about everything that he knows, but no one would show interest, which would make the person think that no one wants his help. But people *do* want help and information. As soon as I start talking with people, they ask questions. They *want* to know about spirituality, about Law of Attraction, investment, retirement, about purpose and passion, about the ashram. People want to expand their knowledge and their life experience. They want to be inspired. And some want more than that. Some want to take action and get involved. So, saying yes and being creative and open to what comes always serves me.

I think curiosity and creativity were always within me. They just took a long time to blossom. Circumstances brought all of it to the surface for me to see it and nurture it. We all have that inner creative knowing, and we have more capacity than we show to the world, or are aware of, because we don't know how. All of the circumstances of my life slowly brought out what had been hibernating inside of me, unrealized. Also—*for those who believe*—all of the experiences in my past lives contributed to the human I am in this life. Just because we don't remember past lives doesn't mean we didn't have them. I don't remember mine, but I have clues, indicators, and abilities. We all do. It took everything that happened to me to become aware of who I am. With every "Yes," it just keeps evolving and expanding.

# Chapter 10

# The Law of Attraction In My Life

*"It is the combination of thought and love which forms the*

*irresistible force of The Law of Attraction."*

Anonymous

I talk a lot about The Law of Attraction. It's been one of the biggest forces of positive change and contribution in my life. I'm in the space now where I'm not out there looking for things, just surrendering and allowing the universe to flow to me. When I'm inspired by ideas or presented with opportunities or curious about something, I act immediately, and things show up. I don't search for anything, because I know that everything is connected. Somewhere, someplace, there's going to be a connection to something or someone I desire or need. When I expand myself—*through my imagination, spirituality, vitality, interests, self-expression, networking, or generosity*—my vibrational frequency rises, and the universe matches it. That's The Law of Attraction at work.

Saying yes without thinking too much always pays off, especially when you pay attention to the signs that come up along the way.

Signs are always there for you, even if you haven't learned to see them or trust them yet.

When I was a junior in college at UCLA. I was being interviewed by a life insurance agent. They try to sell policies from the angle of convincing you to get one when you're young because they're cheaper than when you're older. I had declared my college major in chemistry, but then the agent told me that being a chemist shortened my life longevity and my premium would be higher. That was my sign: *You're not going to live that long as a chemist, because you'll accumulate all those chemicals in your body and maybe even blow up in a lab explosion, so you'd better get the Hell out of that life plan.* Even though math and science were my strengths, I had to get out of chemistry.

In talking with my roommate about it, he suggested that I go into accounting. His brother-in-law was working for a Japanese CPA in Orange County, California, who was looking for a Japanese-speaking CPA. I spoke better English than his brother did, though not by much. I hadn't learned until I moved to the US and played with my English-speaking cousins on the farm. The rest of my learning had come on the job. But I was confident enough to make the switch.

UCLA didn't have an undergraduate accounting program, so I couldn't get my degree in accounting, but they had a lot of accounting courses for graduate students. We were on a quarter system, and taking ten-week accelerated accounting classes would allow me to finish faster than if I had taken them in an accounting program. This would actually speed up my education. Convinced. I changed my major to accounting.

In June of 1970, fresh out of college, I was drafted into the military. It was the height of the Vietnam war. Your Military Occupation (MO) is determined during your military interview. Though my degree was in chemistry, I didn't want them to put me in that box, so I really pushed the fact that I was an accountant-bookkeeper, that I had completed all the courses, and that I had held jobs in accounting and bookkeeping. Because I spoke up for myself, my military recruiter classified my MO as an Accountant Specialist. That classification enabled me to be placed in the Military Intelligence Group, which was set up on an island in Pearl Harbor Hawaii, not Vietnam. That was the first miracle. The second was that Pearl Harbor didn't have adequate facilities for us, so we ended up being housed off-base in Waikiki, Honolulu, Hawaii. It was like I was on a tropical vacation.

A guy I met during basic training had a Master's Degree in chemistry from UCLA and was doing his PhD graduate study. The Military Intelligence Group that I was in had no use for a chemist, so he ended up in Vietnam. Out of the five thousand people I was in basic training with, only two of us made it to Hawaii. Had I not changed my major to Accounting and pushed that in my interview, I would have been in Vietnam. Who knows how that would have turned out? By paying attention to the signs, The Law of Attraction provided miracles for me, and I never had to find out.

The Law of Attraction works in its own time, in its own way, and it doesn't work in a straight line. An example of that is when I attended a BNI Conference that BNI members from all over the world came to. We attended an assortment of breakout sessions to learn about different areas of business. I brought two ladies who usually attended these kinds of events with me. Before we arrive, I always tell them, *"Once we get there, I don't want to see you again. We already know each other, and I want to network to meet new people, so don't sit next to me. Scatter and do your own thing."*

The first gathering was a general session with everybody in the same room. When the two ladies came in, I was sitting next to a high-level BNI member from England. They asked if they could sit in the open seats at the end of my row, which was fine. But at the end of that session, we all went to different breakout rooms, and one of the ladies came in and sat right behind me, not realizing I was in front of her. After networking with a gentleman and a new group I met, I stood up to head out to another breakout session, but the group asked me to stay in the room we were in for the next breakout session. I agreed to stay. They wanted to move to a different area of the room, so we found new seats. Lo and behold, the same lady was sitting in the row we sat in, right next to the gentleman I had met from England. As I looked over, I saw a mirror image of the scene where I had been sitting next to him in the beginning. Regardless of my advance preparation for separating from the two ladies, unintentionally, they ended up being in the same room as me.

Here's a related story of how The Law of Attraction works without effort. The group I'd been talking with at the conference wanted to plan a future get-together. In agreeing, I mentioned that I had met a lady at another BNI meeting who might like to join us, and they told me to invite her.

The following week, I was scheduled to present at our BNI meeting. The woman I was going to invite happened to walk into the meeting. I hadn't invited her yet to join me in the future get-together with the other group, and she didn't know that I was presenting at the meeting or where I was sitting. She hadn't seen me, because I was away from my seat, preparing, but she sat down right next to my chair. The Law of Attraction was making the connections without my effort.

People who don't understand The Law of Attraction or believe that LOA is a true law of the universe usually ask, *"Without doing something, or goal setting, or planning my day or future, how do I get what I need to survive and be successful?"*

Things move and flow seamlessly and take care of themselves, one way or another, through The Law of Attraction. It's a vibrational magnet type of energy that is operating and present all of the time. Unlike the law of gravity, or other laws of physics, none of us were taught about LOA or the other universal principles. But, just because you don't know something or believe something exists, doesn't mean it doesn't exist. You'll see the signs.

Being the multi-tasker that I am, I sometimes trade while I'm driving, which can be pretty distracting. It's usually not a problem, because I take the same routes wherever I go, and I know where everything is. Last week, the route I normally take had a detour, and I had to go around and come back a different way. That landed me in a location I wasn't familiar with, so I didn't see the big center divider when I turned left, and I ran right into it. The front bumper of my Tesla was suddenly dragging down the street. I don't get bothered by things like that, though. My son-in-law is a mechanic. He tied it up for me, which worked for a short time until the fan started making noise. I could still drive it, but I immediately thought to myself, *"Ok Sam, this is a sign from the universe. It's time for a change."*

My other son-in-law is my go-to guy for tech, trading, and car intel. He's the one who introduced me to the Tesla in 2019 when he and I both purchased one. For me, it was time for a change meant that it was time to order a new Tesla. I decided to give my older one to my son-in-law so that my younger daughter could commute to work and not have to pay for gas. He had introduced me to the trading group that helped me make a lot of money, including Tesla stock earnings, so this would be my thank-you gift.

At that point in my decision, what I didn't expect was losing one point five million dollars in trading (so I thought at the time). So, the day I thought I had lost that money, I told my son-in-law that I was going to cancel my Tesla purchase until I sold some real estate to make the money I needed for the car. He'd have to wait a little while before I could give him my older Tesla. As it turned out, when I realized my miscalculation, and then the stock ended up bringing me a return, I didn't need to cancel the Tesla order after all.

With that situation taken care of by the universe, my dilemma was to figure out how to keep my wife from finding out that I bought another car. She hates that I buy something whenever I want it, and she has to wait for what she wants, like new landscaping. So, I ordered my new Tesla in the exact same model and color as my older one, so that she wouldn't notice that I had a new car. When I gave my old Tesla to my son-in-law, I told him that he could not bring it to my house, because that would place two identical Teslas in my driveway. Tesla had a lot of upgrades in the three years since I bought my first one, but the changes are things like a larger motor and longer battery life, so they don't show on the outside. What does show is the slightly fancier style and different color wheels. As long as he doesn't bring my old one to my house, my wife will never know. That's me playing with the Law of Attraction.

I see how the universe is always orchestrating everything to work out. It doesn't all happen in order or the way we think it should, or will. We have to let go, and it just works for us. Because my daughter and son-in-law introduced me to the silver bullet of trading companies, I made money on Tesla stock, and I was able to make money trading again. Even though I thought I was in a very unstable situation, thinking I lost a ton of money and running my car into a center divider, I didn't have any anxiety or get all bent out of shape. My other son-in-law was able to fix my three-year-old Tesla. Instead of losing one point five million, I made sixty thousand, and I was able to buy a new Tesla and give my old one to my daughter and son-in-law.

I see how it all plays out. So, I don't need to worry about being taken care of, or put effort into trying to manage life. No matter what choice I make, I don't worry about thinking I might have made a bad choice. I can change my mind, or stay on course and just allow life to bring things to me. When an opportunity comes by, it's not *should I or shouldn't I, or what if?* It's Yes! I don't have to think about what to do. My response is immediate. And when catastrophe hits, I don't get all bent out of shape. Life is kind of a game that you can play if you know the way it works and keeps your vibrational frequency high and your heart open.

The more I cleaned my mindset and my body, the higher my frequency rose, and life began presenting me with people on a higher frequency to match me. In energy vibration, like attracts like. The Law of Attraction continues to draw in people and situations in the same or similar frequency. Sometimes, the way this manifests is that meeting one person opens a doorway of unexpected connections. Some of the people I met were involved in the natural health industry and focused on learning about anti-aging, holistic living, and energetic health products and practices. Others were healers and psychics.

One of the people I attracted and have stayed connected with is Jan Edwards. I met her in 2013 when she was invited as a guest to our BNI chapter meeting. She put on holistic health fairs for companies and was the founding president of the Orange County Chapter of the Holistic Chamber of Commerce. I joined her chapter and was then invited to join her Holistic Mastermind group, which focused on energetic manifestation and the Law of Attraction. I met Matt Finch at one of these mastermind meetings, who became a mentor in my Plant A Seed Institute nonprofit. In 2017, when I needed help promoting Plant A Seed, I enlisted Jan's ghostwriting and marketing on social media. Then, in 2019, I wanted to help my guru Valji promote his medical yoga in the US, so we participated in one of Jan's employee holistic health fairs. In 2021, I received one of her quarterly newsletters, which prompted me to decide to write my autobiography, and I contacted her to help me write it. This is just one example of how one connection can link to expanding in other areas.

Another example is when I was introduced to a holistic health technology product called Healy, by a woman who also invited me to attend a Wake-Up OC networking meeting. By attending that meeting, I ended up buying an amazing health product called Avacen. Through Wake-Up OC, I met a lot of great and supportive people. This one connection alone is blowing open a portal of new opportunities for me that I wasn't expecting.

Investments provide connections too. Shortly after I invested in a company that sells wine and tequila, the company creators became interested in working with me on a joint project to promote not only their products but also my sound-healing wine glasses.

The more I opened myself to understanding spirituality and energy, and the more I worked with The Law of Attraction to keep my frequency high, the more people I met who had psychic and healing abilities. It feels like I'm surrounded by these people with extraordinary human abilities.

One of them became a good friend. She has the gift of seeing. When I focus on someone, she receives an energetic feeling and information and can tell me what kind of person she or he is, personality characteristics, whether to associate with him or her and even whether to go into business with him or her. I don't have to say the name of the person or give any details. She doesn't usually need anything. In fact, it's sometimes better if she doesn't know anything.

One of her clients was a large company that had been embezzled by a million dollars. The company had hired a forensic accountant who produced a fifty-page document of his investigation, but he wasn't able to identify the embezzler. So, the company called in my friend. Without reading or seeing the accountant's investigation file, only a stack of purchase invoices, she was able to point to a line on one of the invoices and advise the company to track that line to find the individual. They did, and they caught him.

My friend, Matt Finch, introduced me to the mystic healer, Sonja Grace, who is known by millions. She refers to herself as a Spirit traveler. One of her gifts is being able to temporarily dissolve her physical body and travel to the center of the universe, to a previous time. Her guides literally take her from one place and time and bring her to another. Most people don't believe this is possible, but when you learn that time is not linear but spherical with layers of different times, realms, and dimensions, you understand that there is no past or future time. It is all happening simultaneously in the present.

Sonja and I met in Los Angeles at a couple of events she was presenting at in early 2020. I have a photo of us standing together there, under a light shining down on both of us. But, in the photo,

68

the light is only shining on her, not me.

Recently, I met another interesting psychic who used her gift to uncover an underground toxic leak at one of the Irvine Company properties. As a result of her discovery, they hired her to work for them.

In a phone consultation, I had with another psychic, I mentioned my ashram. She tuned right into it and confirmed that it will be built. She told me that the location will be in Trabuco Canyon and that the government will donate the land to me. What she didn't know was that my partner and I had already decided to build it in Trabuco Canyon.

One of the amazing memories of the Law of Attraction in my life is my trip to Mount Fuji. In 2019, a friend asked if I wanted to take a trip to Japan, but I told him that I was already planning to go and wanted to make the trip alone. He mentioned that there was a possibility of him going again in the summer, because he wanted to climb Mount Fuji, and asked if I wanted to join him. I said yes. I shared my plan with my daughter and her husband, and they were interested in going too. So, the four of us decided to do the Mount Fuji climb as soon as the season opened in the first week of July, to be sure to get a good tour guide.

Soon after, my son-in-law discovered that he had a commitment that first week and couldn't go, unless we went in the second week of July. But, my friend had a major work contract during the middle of July and couldn't go unless we went at the end of July. With everyone's availability accommodated, we rescheduled our trip for the end of July, with an agreement that we do the climb up on a Friday and descent on Saturday, so that our flight arrangement would be more convenient. However, by the time we were finally ready to book our trip, the Friday and Saturday climb-up and back dates had all been reserved. With no other choice, we booked the climb up on the last Thursday and the descent on the last Friday of July.

Here's where The Law of Attraction began its magic. If we had gone with our original plan during the first week of July, I would have missed the opportunity to connect with four brand-new health practitioners who showed up that week and began preparing me for the trip. One was an essential oils distributor. On my prior trip to Mount Whitney, I had major issues with altitude sickness, so consulting with her helped me integrate the use of certain oils and applications and prevented me from having altitude sickness. Another practitioner introduced me to ASEA Redox molecules. In climbing down the mountain, you use muscles that you don't typically use, so you usually feel quite a lot of pain for a few days after the descent. But, the ASEA helped my immune system, and I had no muscle pain during or after the climb. A third practitioner was an intuitive chiropractor who worked on me to get ready for the hike, adjusting my spine and strengthening my alignment and muscles. The fourth was a distributor of Bemer, which is a microvessel stimulator for blood flow. Using it improved my circulation in the extreme altitude and temperature conditions, and I have been using it in my morning health regime ever since.

If I had made the trip anytime during the first half of July as originally planned, I would have missed all of these health benefit angels who prepared my body for the climb. As a result of all the treatments I got from them, I had zero pain, which was almost a miracle for a seventy-two-year-old. For the first time, climbing was not difficult, and I felt great.

But that wasn't the only outcome of the Law of Attraction on that trip. There was an avalanche on Mount Fuji, so all scheduled climbs were shut down that first and second week of July. If we had gone during either of our first two date choices, we would have traveled to Japan and not been able to do the climb. Of course, our money would have been credited toward a new date, but we wouldn't have been able to stay longer and do it. The universe had been orchestrating the way for us.

There was one more magic trick presented to us. The Mount Fuji climb is a two-day event, with the first half of the climb on day one and the final ascent on the second day. Typically, the last half of July is typhoon season in Japan and extremely rainy, which would have made the climb up and down more difficult, and possibly dangerous, or even cause a closure. It never rained on our ascent. And, we reached the summit just in time to view a spectacular sunrise. A doughnut-shaped cloud had formed, with a hole in the middle, and right at sunrise, the sun popped up in the middle of the cloud, perfectly centered in the doughnut hole. The sun and cloud stayed in that formation for about thirty seconds, just enough time for my daughter to take her iPhone out of her backpack and capture the scene. Immediately after she took the shot, the sun shifted. Three minutes later, the sky started pouring buckets of rain and drenched us. It was like the universe was saying, *I'm creating perfect timing for you to see my beautiful art.*

Here's the cherry on top. The next day, as we toured various places in our taxi, I was talking with the driver about our descent from Mount Fuji. He told us that we were lucky that we came down the day before, because the typhoon was coming on Saturday, and the mountain would be shut down. If the Friday and Saturday reservations had not all been booked, we would have been stranded at the top of the mountain on Saturday, unable to come down.

That's why I call it magic. The Law of Attraction worked all these components, without our effort or worry, and all in perfect timing. We didn't have to figure things out or even get what we thought we wanted. The universe was making sure we did not miss out on anything by putting roadblocks in the ways we thought would get us what we wanted, to redirect us to the path that would actually give us what we wanted. It's crazy to think of all the maneuvering that universal energy did to make this trip so easy and successful for us. So many parts came together. Even if one of the elements had changed, nothing would have unfolded the way it did. None of us was in pain or got injured or got stuck or got left. Nothing negative happened. It was seamless, even though it may not have looked that way in the planning stages. That's how it works.

The after-effects of contemplating this and realizing how everything played out catapulted my belief system through the roof. Any doubt of what I had previously thought was impossible was erased from my beliefs. That whole experience was a powerful message from the universe that came in loud and clear. We did the right thing. I was on track.

We can't possibly know how it will come together. We just have to have faith and know that it will and surrender. If you get into the place of what I call total non-resistance, and you allow life to guide you, you will be taken care of. Everything will happen for you. You never doubted that you would learn to walk by yourself. You just followed your inner nudges and desires, and you walked. You never worry that you might be sucked off the earth and spin in space. There are universal laws working all the time without your need to control them. Just like gravity.

**The Law of Attraction Further Explained**

LOA: An energetic principle, like gravity. You attract from the universe (world/life) the people, circumstances, and things that are on the same heart energy frequency (emotion) you are.

What you focus on, you get. You attract from the universe and the world the people, circumstances, and things that are on the same energy frequency as you are. If you focus on something negative, you attract negative, through the universe responding back to you in like energy, in the form of negative people, circumstances, or things.

Frequency is an energy that can be measured. David Hawkins, the author of *Power Versus Force*, performed an analysis of a few spiritual leaders and compared their frequency with that of the common man. He used an energy frequency scale that measured the life force energy. The outcome of his analysis measured the frequency of Jesus and Buddha at about 1000, Mother Teresa at around 700, and most common people below 200. His analysis concluded that an energy frequency measurement of 200 or higher was the lowest frequency of a person with no trauma or strife. A person whose frequency measured under 200 always attracted negative internal and external issues, like accidents, abuse, health problems, mental imbalance, pain, loss, relationship conflicts, poverty, and other struggles.

A friend of a friend came to my house one night. She didn't want to park on the street in front of my house, because she believed that her car might get hit, stolen, or robbed. She had experiences of people running into her car, breaking into her car, and causing other damages to her car. She wanted to park in the driveway because she believed it would be protected there. What she didn't know was that the low frequency of her thoughts and beliefs was what had attracted those circumstances to her. She has high intelligence and character, but those measurements of intellect and morals don't guarantee a high energy frequency. Her thoughts and beliefs were so negative and fear-based that they lowered her energy frequency and created a downward spiral of her entire life and career. By the time we met, she was nearly homeless.

This might seem sad to most people, but when you understand how everything works and the mechanics of the energy of the universe and our reality, you're not sad. You finally see how you are in control of what happens to you and what ceiling you put on your desires. Your emotional vibration or energy frequency is connected to the depth of your heart, the mastery of your thoughts, your emotional freedom, your level of appreciation, and your ability to trust, tune into, and flow with your internal guidance in each present moment.

This can't be explained to people who don't understand, because they're not in the space (perspective, mindset, consciousness) of being able to understand. So, they'll just get frustrated or upset when you try to teach them, which will make things worse for them. Most people don't do anything to drastically change their beliefs or lifestyle until something really bad happens—and even then, many don't change. Most people need to reach a point of so much discomfort or catastrophe in their world that they finally are willing to ask for help and surrender to whatever that looks like. Usually, their heart has to break open enough that they're open to making a change, even a complete transformation.

Once you get to that inspired, heart-opening higher energy place and vibration, everything changes for you. When I got there is when all the creative ideas and thoughts began to come. Before I changed, I couldn't have cared less about this knowledge or way of thinking and those kinds of people. I wouldn't have made time to listen or understand any of that. That's why those ideas and people never came in. I didn't open myself to it. Now I do. Now I create time to practice keeping my energy frequency high and my heart open. And I attract new, higher-vibration people all the time.

The universe is always on course and always matching the frequency of the vibration that you're in. That's why I say that psychiatry never works because you're focusing on the situations, people, beliefs, and emotions that you experienced in the past. When you do that, you take all of that in again, as if they were real again and happening again to you now. Then, as the universe matches your energy, it sends people and situations with the same prior low energy to you, and you feel the same cycle you did back then. It's hard to shake it. Going back to dive into the past can actually spiral downward and make you feel worse than you did before you started. But when you focus on the present and the positive and the possibilities, the Universal Divine frequency matches that frequency and sends people and situations with that energy to you. And the spiral can go upward and get better.

Whether you believe me or not, or understand this or not, you can't hide from the universal laws, just like you can't pretend there's no such thing as gravity. You're totally exposed to them, all the time. The universe feels you and where you're at in every moment. But, it doesn't hear your words. It feels your frequency vibration, your heart, and your energy. You can say, *"I love you."* But if you don't fully mean it, your energy frequency is not at the love frequency, and the universe doesn't feel the love vibration from you. So, it doesn't respond back to you with things and people at the love vibration. It also works the opposite way. If you say negative words or phrases, but in a heartfelt place of peace, love, or appreciation, the universe feels the energy of heart, peace, love, or appreciation, and responds by sending people and things in that energy to you.

The Universe wants to help you. It always rights itself. It wants to fulfill your dreams. It wants you to feel and act from your true energetic power and brilliance. The way you receive that help is by just being happy. If you are sincerely happy or joyful, your energy frequency vibration will be at the highest level. How do you get into a space of a happy or joyful vibration? Connect with something that you fully, truly love, appreciate, feel grateful for, or feel joy in. That place of high frequency opens the door to things happening seamlessly for you, without effort. The universe always provides and always responds to the frequency.

People say that this explanation is too simple. That's where the main trouble started. We were taught that life is hard and that things aren't easy, and that you have to prove yourself and work hard and do certain things to have a good life. None of that is true. Life is simple. It's simple in that you only have to do that one thing, be in a frequency of happiness (love, appreciation, gratitude, joy, fun). Maintaining that frequency is the difficult thing, only because we were taught that it's hard. When you were a toddler, you were full of joy and fun and laughter and love. Life was simple. How do you remember how to be that on a daily basis, on a moment-to-moment basis? That's the journey back to remembering who you really are, all one, all love, all connected. It's up to you to learn that so that you can regain and maintain your high vibration.

That's why I do the things I do every morning and throughout the day. That's why I talk the way I talk. My growth and energy fine-tuning has been an ongoing process over the last sixteen years. It's based on meditation, heart connection, and what's between the ears (attitude). All of that has contributed to who I am today. I keep growing, and the evolution of what I'm being and doing is all aligned with my life purpose. It never ends. It'll keep evolving forever. Learning that and maintaining that is part of my evolution. It's part of my mission. And the more I do that, the more things show up without any effort on my part. The Universe and The Law of Attraction take care of me.

To work with The Law of Attraction, you have to be listening. And you can't be closed-minded. The universe is constantly giving us signs, but if we don't listen, we don't hear them. Then, we don't make the connections, and the opportunities pass right by us. I could have ignored the signs. I could have not concerned myself with any of that information, which was a high possibility for me, because I was left-brained. Math and science were my strengths, not creative quantum possibility thinking.

But, I *did* listen. I started listening without knowing why when I was in college. Even though I was young and not consciously looking, that interview with the life insurance agent triggered me to make a life-altering decision. If I hadn't made that life plan change, I would have spent my life working in a lab somewhere, inhaling chemicals. I could have been dead by now. That one decision changed my career path. And I've been hearing and seeing the signs ever since, though there were many years when I didn't. I'm always listening now.

I'm walking in a space of inspiration. In that space, there's really nothing I need to do. When you're ambitious, you're *trying* to *do* things, in order to get things. But, when you're inspired, the universe is operating to do things *for you. Things just show up for you.* That's the space I've been in, and I see through the lens of my experiences that it's all accelerating. It's actually happening more and more.

I had a copy of the photo my daughter took of the sunset over Mount Fuji enlarged, and I hung it on the wall in my office to remind myself what to pay attention to. I look at it every morning when I do my daily spiritual practices. It is the proof that reminds me that anything is possible. I'm totally committed to living in this knowing. It is real, like gravity, but way more fun.

# Chapter 11

# Know Thyself

*"To know yourself as the being behind the thinker,*

*the stillness underneath the mental noise,*

*And the love and joy underneath the pain,*

*is freedom, salvation, enlightenment."*

Eckhart Tolle

They say that you are the average of the five people closest to you, including yourself. I understand that and see the validity of it. That would have been truer in my thirties, forties, and fifties, before my spiritual awakening and when I wanted to be liked. However, in observing the people I've been connected with over the past couple of decades, I see that there aren't many similarities I have with any of them.

I definitely would not describe myself as common. There are some, like me, who don't have five, or four, or even three or two people that they are "close to." We are the ones who don't follow, who don't people please, who don't need to be followed, but have an independent, unique way of thinking and being that guides them internally.

Of course, I wasn't always this way. All of the experiences each of us have, from birth through our entire life, make us who we are. At the age of seventy-five, after fifteen years of deep awakening and evolution, I am completely different from the person I was for most of my life. I'm not a believer in going back to the past, but like your life purpose, your identity is continually changing and evolving. All former versions of me contributed to who I am today, so I'll share a bit from my younger years.

I'm kind of a dichotomy. While a large part of me is quick to laugh and doesn't take life seriously, another part of who I am is like the Samurai, focused and able to stay somewhat unemotional to life's situations. This was woven into my DNA, but the fearlessness of the Samurai didn't kick in until I moved away from home. I suppose that's when I began to wonder what role I played, and what I was made of.

To discover that, I had to start opening myself up to the world. All that stifled energy from being muted needed somewhere to express itself. I wanted freedom. I wanted to feel good. I wanted to be unbounded. I wanted to lift the limitations. But first, I had to find where they were. Much of my life was about testing my internal and external limits, and I did that in a variety of ways over several decades, some of which I shared in the earlier chapters of this book.

At twenty-two, I was drafted into the military. I didn't want to go, so I purposely answered all the questions incorrectly on the written test. The draft center officer said to me, *"You've got to be pretty smart to get a zero."* For the hearing test, you are instructed to click the button as soon as you start to hear the tone through your headphones. I waited. One, two, three, four. Then I clicked the button. The officer asked me, *"Are you hard of hearing?"* I looked at him and said, *"What?"* He asked me again. I told him that I was in a band and that all that noise affected my hearing.

I never played in a band. He caught on to me and initiated a completely different set of tests that I couldn't fake. I was so mad that when I got home, I called the draft center and screamed, *"I planted a bomb! You better get the Hell out of there!"* That was before cell phones, so they couldn't trace the call. Even if they did, I'm not sure that would have deterred me.

In my third or fourth year as a CPA, I had to take a continuing education seminar in Las Vegas. I had a Corvette at the time, and I wanted to see how fast it could go, and how fast I could make the trip. I left early in the morning. I saw signs along the way indicating aerial radar, but I ignored them. I didn't care. I had my mind made up, and I went balls out. Averaging one hundred twenty miles an hour, weaving through the traffic, I took that car so fast that it skipped up off the freeway. I didn't know what compelled me. It was spontaneous. Most people would be afraid of getting a ticket, being thrown in jail, or getting into an accident. I never thought about the consequences. I was a fearless adventurer—and ornery. I usually don't do anything I don't want to do.

The energy behind my orneriness was aggressive and wild and wanted attention. In the earlier years, I did crazy things from an ego place, needing to be liked. It led to drinking and acting crazy, which is what my kids remember from their growing up. They hung out with my friends and me when we played basketball and drank. At my first daughter's wedding, I drank and danced and goofed off so much that, when it was time for my second daughter's wedding, she pleaded with me, *"Dad can you please calm down and not drink so much?"* I drank anyway because my friends encouraged me to. They knew that when I drank enough, I was funny and crazy, and they wanted to see that. I did the same thing at my nephew's wedding. I was not a gentleman, and I had to apologize. Alcohol lowered my inhibitions and revealed the unsophisticated part of me.

Years ago, my wife and I went to Vegas with my golfing buddies and their wives. Before dinner, the women went off on their own, and my buddies and I decided to go up to one of our rooms to drink. We didn't want to spend money on drinks at dinner because we drank quite a bit. So, we got a head start in the room. Actually, we got soused—to the point that I threw up during dinner all over the table, and all over me. My buddy took me to the bathroom to wash myself off, but I didn't go up to my room to change clothes or take a shower. I came back to the table and finished dinner. After dinner, one of my friends wanted to gamble, but the casino was crowded, except for one blackjack table where one person sat alone playing. My friend told me to go sit next to him. Right after I sat down, the man at the table bolted up and left the table. WE all burst out laughing.

On another casino trip, I was gambling for several hours with the same group of friends. Sometime between midnight and dawn, after having quite a few drinks, I left to use the restroom. Not paying attention to the sign above the restroom or anything around me, I walked into the empty restroom and into the stall. I saw the Kotex feminine product dispenser on the stall wall as soon as I sat on the toilet. Realizing that I was in the women's restroom, I heard the clicking of shoes walking in and into the stall on my left. I looked down and saw a garter belt and women's feet in heels and immediately lifted my legs off the floor. I held them up and sat as quietly as I could, praying that she would leave quickly. She left a couple of minutes later, and as soon as I stood up, another set of clicking heels came in. I sat back down and lifted my legs in the air again, hoping she wouldn't try to push the door to the stall that I was in. I held my breath as she went into the stall on the right side of me. The second she left; I bolted out of there.

Through the years, I've become quite a multi-tasker. I like to do more than one thing at a time, so I can accomplish as much as possible and continue to increase my efficiency. This can create some results that I'm not expecting. For example, when I go to the bathroom, I can't just go in there and sit without doing anything else. I always have to bring a book or something with me. There's a story about this that I won't go into here, but you can use your imagination.

In my increasing efficiency, I sometimes take multitasking to the extreme and do it when I'm driving. Because I'm not paying full attention to driving and parking, I sometimes bump into curbs. My rims are all scratched up, and I've had tires blow up. Fortunately, my new Tesla has autopilot, so things aren't as bad as they used to be in my old Tesla.

A major part of who I am is calm, resilient, and easygoing, so dents and tire blows don't bother me. A couple of years ago, I parked my new Tesla in the parking lot to go into the bank. On my way back to my car, I watched as the car next to mine pulled out and hit the side of my car. It left a dent, but I had to be somewhere, so I told the driver not to worry about it, and I got in my car and took off. I imagine that he was probably thinking, *Wow! It's my lucky day.* Those things don't bother me. I like things neat and clean, but if something happens, I'm okay with it. I never got the dent fixed. It's my reminder that it's no big deal.

A strong element of me is my higher perspective that always sees everything that happens as positive, no matter how it looks or feels at the time. Here are two stories that happened within three short days, but the benefit of one of them has lasted to this day.

My friend Pedro and I went to Mexico to visit a cattle farm that his uncle was taking care of. After ending our visit with a five-acre horseback tour of the property, we spent the night in a hotel in Cancun before our morning plane back to the states. In the middle of the night, I got up to use the bathroom and sat on the toilet. I happened to look down and saw that my scrotum was infested with ticks. A group of them had burrowed their way inside, and I could see them through the thin skin. I started squashing them with my fingers, which pierced my skin, and I started bleeding.

When Pedro got up, he saw that he had ticks all over his body, though not in his scrotum. We decided to go to the beach, thinking we'd soak ourselves and get rid of them. But there were so many of them, so we stood on the sand by the water picking ticks off of each other's backs, like two monkeys. I can't imagine what the people on the beach were thinking.

I thought we had gotten rid of them, but after I got home, I saw that there were some still on me. When I got to the office Monday morning, I called one of my doctor clients and told him what happened. He wanted me to come in right away, but I was with a client and I didn't want to interrupt our appointment, so I never went in. My attitude was, *"I don't care; I'm not worried about it; I'll be fine."* That was me being fearless and positive and unworried, like a Samurai. Subconsciously, I might have been thinking that I didn't want him to touch my scrotum. Regardless, I was ok. Within a couple of days, they were all gone.

On my way out of the office that same evening, I saw that the front door to my office had come off the hinges, and I couldn't close it. I decided to spend the night there, to make sure no one came in. I lay on the floor in the hallway of my office and went to sleep. One of my employees who comes in late arrived at about nine that night. When he saw the building door slightly open, he was alarmed and went back out to the parking lot. The parking lot patrol officer was cruising around, so he flagged him down and told him that something was going on in our office. The officer came to the office door, shined his flashlight in, and saw my feet on the floor of the hallway. He told my employee to go back to the parking lot. Not knowing if I was dead, or if a burglar was in the office, he went back to the parking lot and called in the K-9 unit for backup.

When the K-9 backup unit came, they didn't release the dogs, thankfully. My employee gave them the key to the back door of the office, and when they came into the back, their flashlights woke me up. I wondered what was going on and sat up. The officers told me to stay on the floor with my back to them and scoot backwards toward the door. I had to take all my keys and everything out of my pockets and lay them on the floor. They handcuffed me, took me outside, and threw me down on the sidewalk. They never asked me who I was, or if it was my building, to see my identification—nothing.

When my employee came over and saw that it was me, he told them who I was, so they took the handcuffs off and left. But they left with all of my keys, so I had to call the police department and tell him what happened and wait for them to come back and bring my keys.

I was lucky. They had a feeling that something didn't add up, which is why they held off on releasing the K-9 dogs. I would have been attacked if they had, and so would my little dogs that I had been thinking about bringing to stay with me that night. They would have been tortured or killed. But I changed my mind, and they changed theirs. And that's the way it works. Everything turned out positive.

The way they treated me did give me a bad taste for the police department for a while though. A year later, I was called for jury duty. When I was asked by the final group if there is any reason I should not be on the jury, I said, *"Yeah. I shouldn't be on it, because I hate cops."* They asked why. I explained how they had treated me, how they handcuffed me and threw me on the ground in the parking lot without asking me who I was, which was the owner of the business trying to guard my business against intruders and then left with my office keys. After hearing my story, they released me. Because of that, I was able to avoid jury duty that year and every time after that. From my perspective, I'm grateful for the incident at the office. Not having to do jury duty again for the rest of my life saved me from losing time and money being away from my business.

Another positive came out of that night at the office. Every year for about fifteen years, I used to donate five hundred dollars or more to the police department for their protective services. After what they did to me, and did not protect me, or my business by taking my keys, I didn't feel that way anymore. When they called that year to ask me if I wanted to donate, I said no. They asked, *"Why? You've been donating for over fifteen years."* I told them what happened that night at my office, and they've left me alone ever, never calling for a donation. With that, I've saved money every year.

Those three connecting events show all the elements of who I am—positive; crazy; fearless; unconcerned; calm, and landing on my feet in a better place than I was before. They say there are people who see the glass half empty and people who see the glass half full. I see glass all the way full, and always full.

I'm curious and adventurous. I've done a lot of crazy things in my life. I never worried about what could happen. My viewpoint has been, if things happen, they happen. I never looked at the potential consequences. Who would be able to look at all the consequences and still do the things I've done and do? Most people would be too afraid. That's what happens when you think about things too much. When you analyze the future that isn't even real. You think yourself out of doing anything. *What if I lose money? What if I get caught?* You think like that, and you become frozen in fear and anxiety, and you don't do anything. A lot of people get caught in that space, overthinking, and creating future stories that aren't real. Then they can't take action. Or, some do decide to do something and end up getting fined or losing, so they never dare or try anything like it again. Then, they become jaded or take on a victim mindset.

It's the fearlessness in me that knows that it doesn't matter if I get a ticket or a ding in my car. It doesn't prevent me from doing it again, and again, and again. In my earlier years, I did crazy things to be liked. I don't have that need anymore, but I still do things that most people would never do. Being adventuresome, experiencing the thrill of driving fast, and feeling limitless feels good. Fearlessness is the way of the Samurai.

Fearlessness is also a frequency. Fearlessness heightens emotions, releases dopamine, and increases the likelihood of higher-frequency experiences. When you feel good about something, you become more assertive and confident. When you feel more confident and assert yourself, you do a lot of things better. When you do things better, you feel good. When you feel good, your frequency vibrates much higher. When you vibrate higher, the universe responds by giving you good and higher feeling experiences.

By the time I was a year into my first relationship, which happened years later than most people, I felt so much relief, satisfaction, and heart-opening that I was able to loosen the grip my ego's fear and judgment had on my way of being. I became more expressive and relaxed, and I felt better. One outcome of this is that, although I'd been in a bowling league long before I met my girlfriend, after we had been dating for a while, my average score went up forty points.

It is in my fearlessness that I am abundant, out of scarcity. Fearlessness and abundance allow me to feel more peace. I still like to go fast, but I also take time and space to be still. The stillness allows my body, mind, and heart to more finely tune in to one another and the subtleties of energy and people and life.

If there's one thing my kids would never guess about me, that would surprise, or even shock them to discover (which they are as they read this book), it's how deeply involved I am in my spirituality and evolution. The crazy drinking attention-seeker is not who I am anymore, but I don't know whether my kids realize the transition I made, or how I've evolved.

In deciding to tune in to Source and allow myself to keep evolving and drop resistance to perceived limitations, I see how much I've changed. I made a quantum turn and began creating positive things. I also see what has been there from my beginning, and before my beginning, and what remains. A lot of it has to do with peace and compassion. As I've matured and stepped fully into a fearless, positive, and compassionate humanitarian, the Universe responded, *"Because of your life purpose, we're going to keep you on the earth plane for a longer time."* I'm not sure that's exactly the way it happened or the way it actually works, but I feel it.

Allowing my vibrational frequency to stay high is always my primary focus. Anything you do that increases your energy and frequency creates a response from the universe to match you with an increased frequency. Your desires and wants are taken care of. The difficult thing for most people is being able to maintain that high internal frequency when you don't have an external influence, like a girlfriend or some other motivator. If you're making money, you have a partner who loves you, and everything's going great in your external world, you can reach the feel-good level all the time. Can you get to the same feel-good place when you don't have all that? That's the target that I aimed for and finally reached.

I've learned how to maintain that frequency so that external events don't affect me. I feel the Universe looking after me. I learned how to surrender to the energy and pay attention to the indicators, and the Universe responded, *"Because of your frequency, we're going to get you to Hawaii, and you won't have to go to Vietnam."*

Nurturing peace and harmony in my environment has become my primary goal, to raise the vibrational frequency of the spaces I spend the most time in. My office and the separate rooms in it have become the place in which I spend the most time, not only working, but napping, trading, listening to inspirational music and readings, and doing my daily spiritual practices. I brought in a set of plants to my office seven years ago and created additional plants from the cuttings. I don't use fertilizer, only tap water. I arranged the vines to cascade out of the plants down into a large pot. When I bought a singing bowl and started playing it, my plants started thriving. They're so vibrant and crisp in clarity and energy that some people think they're plastic. I intertwined the leaves, so that they are supporting each other to grow upward, reaching for the sky, toward the light, like Atlas carrying the world. Their energy really enhances the vibration of the space.

Nurturing living things—*rather than killing them as I did on the farm growing up*—has become an essential part of my internal and external peace and harmony. Besides my plants, my aquarium friends have been with me for almost eighteen years. One of them swims backwards. For a while, I'd come in the morning before dawn, and she'd look right into my face and then turn around and swim backwards toward me, showing off for me. Kids love my fish. They point to the different ones and say, *"Oh there's Nemo! Oh, there's Dory!"* Their flow and effortless movement in the water reflect peace and ease and harmony, good for relaxation and meditation. My office is like a Garden of Eden. I don't have an apple tree, though, so if you want to reenact the full Garden of Eden scene, bring an apple when you come!

I don't want to give the impression that I'm always serious, balanced, peaceful, and flowing seamlessly through life, but I'm continually evolving. I'm still goofy and fearless. I love to laugh and easily laugh at myself. Helping people see the humorous side of things makes people laugh. I don't take life too seriously, and I stay grounded. I know what's truly important and what's not. I don't sweat the small stuff, and most of it is small stuff. Most people would probably not agree with me, but it's all about your point of view.

A lot of people have called me a Renaissance Man. I've been on both sides of life, the dark and the light. I can relate to almost anyone. I share stories and genuinely love to help. Whether it's hardship, health modalities, spirituality, mountain climbing, coping with suicidal thoughts, career decisions, sports, accounting, networking, understanding the laws of the universe, nonprofits, athletics, manifesting, farming, mentoring, or finding compassion, I love to contribute in the areas I have experience in. I know all the languages of the money, investment, and insurance world, including trading commodities, stocks, options, cryptocurrencies, real estate, insurance licenses, and mortgages.

What I'm not is a Jack of All Trades and Master of None. I've done the research and experienced the results. Rather than tell people what to do, I'm an educator, mentor, and advisor, letting them know what options are available and the diversity of results they might attract. There's one exception to this, which is when I manage investment portfolios for a few clients and their families who don't want to learn and prefer to trust my expertise and guarantee of making money for them.

In all other areas, I advise people to make their own decisions and take ownership of whatever they decide or do. For example, in offering health recommendations, if I told people to take a certain pill, that wouldn't solve anything. They wouldn't have researched the territory for themselves. The more they know about what they're doing, the more the placebo effect kicks in, and they have better outcomes. They are in charge of their outcomes.

Now, I'm interested in determining how best to promote my diverse areas of expertise. I rarely market my holistic accounting business, because my clients come by referral. On the other hand, marketing my other ventures, ideas, investments, visions, and collaborations is what I'm passionate about. For me, social media and online forums aren't effective areas to do that. I need to connect with people face to face. I'm all about in-person connection.

More now than ever, I like who I am, quirks and all, and whom I have become. I'm not set in stone. I'm a work in progress. There's hardly anything that bothers me. Whatever happens or doesn't happen is fine. Either way, I'm not thrown off. I have no expectations, and I don't sweat much, if any, of life's stuff.

# Chapter 12

## Who Am I Today

## Daily Disciplines and Practices

*"Depending on what we do, our habits will*

*either make us or break us.*

*We become what we repeatedly do."*

Sean Covey

Who I am is very much a result of what I commit to and practice every day, my habits and routines. Everything I do is from a holistic (health, natural living, and spirituality) intention and foundation. I don't use an alarm clock to wake up. I wake up automatically. Until recently, if I'd gone out to dinner, I'd get home around eight, sleep for a few hours, and get up around one a.m. If I hadn't gone out to dinner, I'd go to bed at six or six thirty and get up between ten thirty and eleven-thirty that same night. Then, I'd head to the office between midnight and two a.m. and begin my morning practice *(below)*. Afterwards, I'd fall asleep to Wayne Dyer's "The Shift," and get another hour or hour and a half of deep sleep in the back room of my office before walking around four a.m. Recently, however, as a result of taking Avacen, I'm usually able to sleep a full eight hours without getting up in the early morning.

For my morning spiritual practice, I meditate and do yoga stretches for an hour. After a shower, I change clothes and go to the office. As soon as I get in, I make two cups of coffee, adding a little coconut oil and one cube of dark chocolate in each. Then, I respond to all my emails. This habit is from a need to clear clutter, including messages, so I go through all of my messages first thing and get it done. Before beginning work on my clients' tax returns, I hook my Bemer up to my back for my micro vessel stimulant session and I take Avacen, which infuses my body with oxygen. After an hour or so, I move the Bemer to my front, and when that session is complete, I put the Bemer LED light on my face.

Then, I turn on the light above my Sunrise Over Mount Fuji picture on my wall, to illuminate it while I listen to a YouTube video of "Amazing Grace" by Cecilia. She's ranked third in the world for her high-tone voice. The color scheme of blues, reds, yellows, and grays in her video is identical to the color scheme of my sunrise picture. I energetically merge the video and the picture into myself by waving my arm in the infinity sign. I finish the video in a meditation pose to tune into the sound.

At the end of the video, I turn on Wayne Dyer in the background and start my reading practice, which includes: Mike Dooley's *"Notes from the Universe;"* *"A Course in Miracles;"* Sonja Grace's *weekly updates;* *"Law of Attraction;"* and *"Tao de Ching."* After my readings, I stimulate all of my chakras with my special frequency-energized wine glass. Then, I stand in front of my Sunset Over Mount Fuji picture and surround myself with the frequency of the sound of the Universe (God) by simulating the sound of *"I Am that I Am"* with my tuning fork.

The tuning fork is really powerful. I sent one to a lady who provides massage and various therapies for the elderly. In response to it, she sent a message back, *"Oh my God! I used this with my patients, and they're healed. The people who couldn't walk are starting to walk!"*

After the tuning fork simulation, I sit in front of my aragonite pyramid, which emits a frequency that neutralizes and wards off any EMF (electromagnetic fields) in my body. I also set a large aragonite coaster under my fruits and vegetables and under my water. I have another under my bed at home to put me in a REM state of sleep, to help me produce lucid dreams. Since I've been using it, I've been having lucid dreams, sleeping more deeply, needing less sleep, and feeling more awake. It's an amazing product. A lady I met at a Wake-Up OC meeting gave me a supplement formulation that also puts me in a REM state, so I'm having even more lucid dreams, and I remember them the next day.

When I finish sitting at the aragonite pyramid, I stand below the sunset picture and make the crosses of Heaven on Earth and do a purification visualization. I envision a blue sky and water coming out of Mount Fuji, down through the forest, dripping over the forest animals, out into a pool of water, then down in a waterfall, and pouring out over me. I visualize it pouring over my crown chakra, then my pineal gland, through my throat chakra, into my heart chakra, flowing down to my solar plexus chakra, into my sacral chakra, through my root chakra, down my legs, then cascading out of my feet and hands, into the Earth. As it goes through me, it detoxifies everything in my body and recycles it into the core of the earth. I end my session with prayers to Mother Earth.

A large part of my morning spiritual practice is being in gratitude. The state of appreciation is one of the highest frequencies that creates positive experiences and abundance. The two spiritual teachers that I am most grateful for have transitioned, but I still communicate with them every morning. One of them had a sign in his home that said, *"As above, So below."* At the time I saw it, I didn't yet know what it meant. That was before I began my spiritual awakening. Now I know. And now I see that, as my teachers who are no longer on the earth plane are doing their work above, I am doing my work below. *As above, So below.*

At six-thirty a.m., I transition into my day trading mindset. I set four iPhones on my desk (like having four computer screens), each connected to different things going on. One displays a set of charts; one shows the list of stocks ready to be bought and sold; one is set up to send emails, and the other one is the one I use to talk with the advisor recommending different stocks to buy and sell. Sometimes, I follow their recommendations, but many I choose on my own. I actually need about six phones to do it really well, so that I can be ready to respond to all of them and dedicate one or two to emails of information and recommendations. Waiting even one second makes a big difference. Eventually, I'll buy two more phones.

When day trading ends around ten thirty, I continue with my work at the firm, managing emails, tax returns, and other work. After work on Monday, Wednesday, and Friday afternoons, I do yoga with my yogi, Valji, and one of my employees. Afterwards, we treat ourselves to a ceremonial glass of wine in my custom-made energetic wine glasses and a little cheese, and exchange ideas and celebrations.

I'm getting to a place where a backlog of work is developing, which I never had before. That's abundance. But, I'm not jumping into any perceived sense of urgency to get it done. There are so many new activities, groups, and connections showing up to add to my days. I always get done what needs to get done in a day.

Caring
Passive
Ambitious
Multi-tasking
Compassionate
Not conditional
Emotionally cool
A lover of laughter
Entrepreneur minded
Unbothered by anything
Free of expectations of others
Passionate about health products
Open to trying anything and everything
Concerned about the world at a macro level
Always looking forward to continually evolving
A frequent experiencer of goosebump moments
Continually inputting and receiving new information
Curious about new ideas, health, gadgets, and projects
Aggressive (day trading, seeking, & trying new things)
A simultaneous player in both passive and aggressive worlds
Continually adjusting my habits and actions for greater efficiency
In bewilderment, innocence, appreciation, & thankfulness for all that shows up

# Chapter 13

## Belief and Beyond

## The Universe, Nothingness, Oneness, The Now

*'In the moment you ask, and believe, and know*

*that you already have it in the unseen,*

*the entire Universe shifts to bring it into the seen."*

Rhonda Byrne

Everything in my life today took root in and manifested my beliefs—my identity, my behavior, my choices, the people, my work, my health, and my daily experiences. My beliefs create my reality. It's all perfect. Everything is happening for me, through the orchestration of Divine Intelligence.

People might argue with my saying that it's all perfect. I believe that God, *or Spirit, Supreme Being, Source, The Divine (or whatever you want to call it)* created the Universe in the Big Bang. When I look at how the world is within the <u>Universe</u>, I see how perfect all of it is—the distance between the Sun and the Earth, the way everything rotates around it, and all the hydrogen and oxygen elements that have to be spewed down onto this place we live in, so that we can have life on Earth. If even one of these elements were off track, life would cease to exist on Earth. God was able to coordinate all of it perfectly. That's the perfection Source was able to create. How else can all of it be possible, but through the perfection of Divine Intelligence?

A lot of people ask, *"If everything's so perfect, why do we have starvation, conflict, violence, pollution, Covid, child abuse, murder, disease, and horrific environmental and government shifts?"* All of that is part of the contrast and duality that has been created in the world, to help us understand all that is. Contrast allows us to see opposites. Without seeing hate, we couldn't know what love is, what love feels like, or what love looks like. We wouldn't appreciate and transform from it as we do without knowing how special it is. There has to be a contrast.

It's the same with life and death. When someone passes at a young age, it might sound and feel horrible, but that person's passing always happens for a reason. The reason might be a sign that the family member or observer needs, in order to get to a place of understanding, change lifestyle, find compassion, or begin an inner transformation. Many people who experience the death of a loved one find it so difficult that they never live in peace and joy again. They let their grief poison and cripple their body and relationships. They take their grief to the grave.

People who understand and have higher wisdom know that the person who passed is going into a place of pure creation. But, we can't tell that to their loved ones who suffer, because they aren't able to hear us. They're in such grief and ignorance about the way things really work. The only way we can help them is by being true to who we are. Sometimes, when we stop trying to explain and convince and encourage, we allow a space of awareness that can flow naturally to them and open them up. That back-off on our part is sometimes an energetic opening that they pick up on and let it move them forward in a new and easier way.

Through the course of studying all of my key spiritual influencers, like Wayne Dyer and Lao Tsu, and by using spiritual tools over the years, I've been inspired to progress to the highest level of evolution, the place of nothingness and oneness. In this place, you see that everything is one. There's no other. There is no separate you and separate me. We are one. Duality disappears. You're part of the oneness that I'm part of. I no longer see any separation. That's the level I'm working toward. I call it *evolving toward the nothingness*.

If we see everyone and everything as "them" and "others," that creates separation from our fellow humans and the greater human experience. It only creates friction and arguments and an inability to see ourselves in the other and the other in us. If we see everyone and everything as Oneness, there is no separation, so there is no other. If there is no other, there is no other to argue with. If there's no other to argue with, there is no argument. If there is no argument, there is no conflict. If there is no conflict, there is no separation. And it's a circle. Everything just flows, because we're all Divine expressions of the Oneness.

There are always external tragedies, but in every event, there's always a positive. We accept those things for what they really are, part of the evolution. The external world does not put me in anxiety or stress. Obviously, I do respond and react to certain situations, but as I continue to evolve toward the highest state of beingness, that reaction will eventually cease. As I move into that place, nothing external that happens will affect my peace of mind. At the place of nothingness, all the noise out there doesn't bother you, because you're in a space of inner peace.

All of this contributes to how you show up right now, your presence right now. The key for each person is to be aware, to be tapped into their heart, and to reflect on what's really going on right here, right now. When you're not looking back at the past or planning the future, you're in the present. That's the now. When you're in the now, you're aware when something is happening within you. When you're aware of the now, you can tap into how you feel. When you can be tapped into your feelings, you receive the truth or clues to the truth of what's really going on under the surface. The nothingness and the oneness support your nowness.

Some people say, *"You are the Universe,"* or *"The Universe is inside you."* What this means is that each of us is a microcosm of the universe, and the universe is a macrocosm of each of us. It's all part of the hologram. Our bodies have trillions of cells, and every single cell is a hologram (duplicate) of the total you. Each cell contains everything that makes up the total you. Someday, they will be able to take that one cell in your body and make another entire you—which they probably already have. That's what a hologram is. All the human beings on Earth are a microcosm of Humanity, and each of us is the hologram of the totality.

"Universe"

All that is, everything in the physical and non-physical worlds, God, Source, Infinity.

The Universe carries you, knows you, loves you, is you.

"Hologram"

The quantum physics principle states that each human is a duplicate of the universe, each human cell is a duplicate of the entire human, and the universe is a duplicate of the human.

"Nothingness"

The absence of words, thought, past or future looking, planning, or doing.

In the state of nothingness—no-thing-ness—you can't see, feel, or touch anything.

"Oneness"

We're all connected.
We can't see the separation, because we're all one, in harmony with each other.

"The Now"

Being completely here and present in the now.

# Chapter 14

# Future Visioning

*"Someone is sitting in the shade today,*

*because someone planted a tree a long time ago."*

Warren Buffet

People always ask me what I'm working on and what's coming up next. I guess I'm a practical creator, always inner-motivated by my desire to create connections and uplift humanity. Living in the present moment, that's when I see a need and come up with practical ways to fill it through my areas of experience, like my Holistic Business Guidance and Plant A Seed Institute. But, it's not only in those. I'm always working in a few areas simultaneously. These are a few other projects on the horizon that I've envisioned over the past couple of years and have been inspired to create.

## Board and Care Facility in Japan

On my 2019 trip to Shimane-Ken, Japan, after seeing the abandoned house that I had lived in when I was born, my cousins pointed out all the homes in the area that were empty and abandoned like mine. They explained that when the resident dies, there's no one to live there, so the family gives the house to the government. The local residents are all aging retirees, getting ready to die. They don't need jobs, so there are no jobs available in the area. With zero commerce, the offspring of the family don't want to live there. They want to live in the city where jobs and younger people live. The government willingly sells abandoned houses for one dollar, as long as the buyer has a plan for the house. A plan includes something that will produce or generate activity, a service to the community, commerce, or revenue.

My mind started incubating an idea. I could convert abandoned homes into board and care facilities, like the ones in the US, but upper-scale, five-star facilities. I'd have one person live in each facility to run it. A fee would be charged to the boarders, not to make a profit, but to pay for their basic needs, and I'd offer scholarships to those who couldn't afford to pay. I would solicit doctors, nurses, and other resource people to come in to help the boarders. Japan already imports Filipinos, who have the skills to take care of the elderly. So, the nurses would invite more Filipinos to come to Japan to teach them how to do that and, in return, the Japanese would teach the Filipinos how to speak Japanese.

I would set up each facility in a nonprofit organization and one hundred per cent financially supported. Japanese Americans here in the US are already living together, isolating themselves from Americans. So, they could move to Japan and bring their friends with them. Selling their house in the US would provide enough money to fund the move into the facility. They could all live together in one community building and be able to retire in their homeland. Their children could come to see them, so they would be with family and cared for.

The government would be in support of it, because it would bring people to Japan and generate commerce, create jobs, and circulate more money. The neighborhood would support it, because it would create jobs for the locals, like carpet cleaners, carpenters, food deliverers, gardeners, caretakers, and other services. When the borders age to a point of needing more than basic care, like medical attention or around-the-clock caretaking, they would be moved to an assisted living center. Building those would also add to the local job force. It would be a win-win-win creation.

Recently, one of my clients was on a Zoom call with a woman in the Japanese community who has an assisted living center in Japan. I gave her an executive summary of my facility. We'll be connecting soon to see what collaboration we can create. When I shared my vision with my psychic friend, Sonja Grace, she tuned in with her guides. They love the idea. The more I pictured the vision, the more certain I felt. I knew it would be supported, and I knew I would attract collaborators. That's how things work in my world.

**Plant A Seed Institute Update**

Plant A Seed Institute is in the process of being revamped. We discovered that mentoring millennials was not working very well and in demand. The updated platform will offer reverse mentoring, with the millennials mentoring the elderly. Seniors have no one to go to when they have questions. Their kids look at them like, *"I don't have time or patience. Why are you so stupid? Why can't you get it?"* In general, their grandkids and younger people typically don't want to hang out with them. For the most part, the age and generational differences are so great that they can't relate.

Millennials and young people know all about iPhones, computers, iPads, and the programs and technology that make up the world today. With help from millennials, the elderly will receive the connection and support they need to function more easily and feel more vital. They will also feel the connection that they are missing from their children and loved ones as they age and become more isolated. For millennials, working with the elderly will provide a feeling of being in service to someone other than their friends and a connection with older generations and values that will open their hearts. There may be only a few millennials who will want to participate, but there is a given three per cent who will have a genuine desire to do it. This generational-spanning mentoring assistance Is another win-win situation. It's all in the works right now.

### The Hundred-Year Tour

The first question people ask someone approaching the age of one hundred or older is, *"What is your secret?"* One of the things I tell people is that Abraham had his first child at the age of one hundred and twenty-five. The Bible even tells us that, during the time of Moses, people lived to be two hundred or more years old. That period of time in the history of mankind seems to be the peak for longevity before it began declining. Looking back a hundred years or more ago, we can see the valley for longevity, before it began to rise again.

There's no telling how high it can rise in the future, or what would keep it from continuing to rise in our present and future generations. We have the information. We have the technology. We have ongoing research. We have proof of energetic anti-aging. For the average person to live to one hundred or older is not out of the question. With gene therapies, consciousness and trauma therapies, Artificial Intelligence, advancing technology, nutrient-dense food and supplementation, stress prevention techniques, and all the health modalities that keep being created, it's more than possible. I feel pretty confident that technology will be there to support more and more people making it to one hundred and older.

Talking with my yogi, Valji, about a way to bring people together in some kind of mission and purpose, inspired the idea of The Hundred Year Tour. I asked him, *"What if we get a group of ten or twenty people together and share our secrets all over the world?"* I thought about having a group of people around my age start a tour, to give people a reason to begin now to do the things necessary for living a long life with health and purpose and involvement. For people who are one hundred years old, plus or minus a few years, being part of a community of others like them would inspire each other to continue. It would also inspire them to talk to other people about it, and the group would expand into a larger and more diverse group of people exchanging ideas and taking inspired action all over the world.

To begin, we'll create a community of like-minded people and form a nonprofit organization for it. Our Zoom calls will connect people from all over, sharing what we do to sustain our health and vitality and enthusiasm for life. We'll tour seven continents with one grand annual tour to build anticipation every year. For lodging and venues, we'll find out which area would welcome and accommodate us. At our tour venues, we'll set up health practitioners and businesses that sell health products. They'll sponsor or donate to our nonprofit in exchange for exposure and promotional testimonials telling how we became so healthy and vital.

The motivation for me is not about me living to be one hundred years old. It's not about me at all. I don't even think about living to a hundred. I just do whatever shows up in my life, as far as ideas, and I just show up. This community doesn't have to wait until I get to that age. I need other people to show up who want to come on board and collaborate and do the research for it. I'll work with others I know, and others I'll meet in the future who will reach the hundred-year mark before I do. Ninety-and ninety-five-year-old people who want to work with me can be the first to begin.

I've never heard of anything like it and, as far as I know, no one's done it yet. I've shared my idea with a few people, and they all resonate with the idea of a tour of one-hundred-year-old people who inspire others with the secrets and health modalities they've used to increase their longevity. I think this could be a project that would get a lot of global attention and gather like-minded people together for a higher frequency humanitarian cause.

My mom died at ninety-seven. My dad died at fifty-one. My oldest sister died at forty-nine. My youngest sister is alive and well at seventy-seven. I'm seventy-five and more vital than ever.

Valji and I joked about selling our sperm because we have good genes for health and longevity. I think sperm is still good at the age of one hundred. People go to sperm banks. Perhaps future mothers-to-be will have a desire to propagate good DNA in their unborn children. Maybe we could make it a fundraiser. With all the anti-aging modalities and technologies, it's possible.

I think the most important factor in living a long life is what's between the ears, your mindset. Your only responsibility is to not let whatever anyone says about you stick to you. If you allow it to, you give it meaning, which gives it value, which gives it power. It then becomes an obstacle to you. If someone gets upset with you and calls you an SOB or something, and you don't accept what he tells you, his energy and words bounce right off you and back to him. Returning to sender, they don't affect you. If you don't take anything personally, it doesn't affect you. It doesn't create anxiety and stress in you, because it has no meaning to you. If you're in that space most of the time, your longevity can increase. This is energy work. This is consciousness. This is part of reversing trauma and conditioning. Living on Earth with zero resistance and zero stress allows you to get to the place where you have a pure, unblocked connection to Source, The Universe, God, or whatever you want to call it. That connection expands your energy and vitality and adds years to your life and life to your years.

Meditation is a good way to get to that space of connection with Source, and to shift any habits of taking anything personally. Go to a quiet place. Take a walk. Hike in nature. Take care of plants. Take care of the fish. Spend time with your pets, or spend time with animals in general. Doing this, or anything that puts you in a place of appreciation or love and nature is the most important and effective way to keep yourself youthful and in high vibration. Do whatever you can to be in that place.

A healthy mindset includes having a belief system that makes you feel good, beliefs that allow you to feel inspired, and habits that maintain a state of feeling good. Some people don't care about looking at their feelings. They don't want to figure them out or do anything about them. Their attitude is, *"I'm not happy. So, what. 'F' you,"* and they just keep going on with their life like that. If that's the kind of attitude you want to have, then that's the kind of life you're going to have. But if you want to make a shift and feel good about yourself and enjoy a long, energized life, you need to start looking at things differently, like what you believe about life that may not be good for you and your happiness, and what beliefs you have that make your life hard.

Living a long and vital life requires feeling satisfied, on purpose, appreciative, and happy. If you're not happy, there's something you need to take a look at. If you don't feel good, maybe you need to think about what happened. Something's not right. Always look at your state of feeling. Looking at how you feel in any given situation is a litmus test to see if whatever you did or didn't do, believe or don't believe, is resonating or not resonating with you. From looking at that, you receive clues that let you know what you want to change and how you want to be in this world, which can lighten and lengthen your life.

We live in the world of energy, vibration, and frequency. A healthy life and happiness raise your vibration, and a higher vibration creates better health and happiness. It's a circle. If you can maintain high emotional energy, or commit to doing whatever it takes to be in the highest frequency and vibration, you will be supporting your longevity. You won't oxidize or wear out as quickly as you will when you exist at a low vibration. The simplest way to do that is to always go to the place of feeling good. If you feel good, you're in the right place, which leads to your longevity and a better chance of living healthfully to one hundred.

**Heaven On Earth Ashrams**

When my yogi, Valji, and I were sharing our thoughts and ideas, we talked about how wonderful it would be to have a health center where we could do yoga. His concept is: *Life is not to suffer, but to celebrate.* During a year of conversations, we started putting the pieces of our ideas and vision together, and the dream of building an ashram was conceived. It's still in creation, but it will be "Heaven On Earth."

The concept is a beautiful place where people can enjoy a pleasant environment to live their final years. On entering, you'll see the sign overhead, *"Heaven On Earth—You've found it!"* All the colors of the rainbow will be visible throughout the property, along with trees and flowers, birds, dogs, cows, and horses. Tiny homes will be available for people who want to buy into the ashram before needing to move there permanently. They'll bring their employees, their families, and their friends to visit and enjoy the facility and its amenities. When they get to retirement age, or when they need some form of assisted living, they'll move in permanently and receive the full spectrum of services from us that they need.

People have lost their connection with the earth. Much of their reality is all sidewalk and concrete, cell phones and computers. Most kids don't know about farming or fruits and vegetables. They think everything grows in the supermarket. Unless they go to the beach, most people hardly even take off their shoes and ground with the earth. Even I rarely go barefoot outside.

At the ashram, the children and grandchildren will feel the attraction to working with the earth, getting their hands dirty, grounding with nature, and giving back to the earth. Grandkids will have fun climbing trees, playing with the animals, and learning how to take care of them. They'll farm, pick fruit, practice yoga, play outside on the peaceful grounds, and enjoy the other activities we'll provide. The ashram will be a beautiful place where kids will want to come and visit their parents and grandparents, aunts and uncles. They'll experience nature and fun and beauty in a peaceful, harmonic community.

The ashrams are not just for people to live in, but can also be a space for weddings, presentations, retreats, health and healing activities, and spiritual events. My big-picture purpose in creating them is to bring people together, to collaborate, and to bring peace on earth.

I'm looking for people who want to collaborate with me and set up "Heaven On Earth" ashrams in different locations. Christy Russ, a woman I have weekly Zoom calls with, wants an ashram on her five-acre compound in Arkansas where she recently relocated from Fountain Valley, California. Another connection I met a few years ago will build an ashram on his property in Trabuco Canyon, California. My psychic friend, Sonja Grace, has been thinking about setting up a retreat space too.

Two weeks before I met Steve Redford, the co-creator of Wake-Up OC, he purchased a property in Bonsall, San Diego, California where he'll build an ashram similar to mine. When I told him about my vision for the ashram, he liked the name and asked if he could use it for his ashram. I gave him permission. I don't try to hoard everything to myself. I don't go to that headspace. I don't worry. Greed, worry, and control never enter my mind. Those ingredients cannot cultivate love, harmony, and abundance.

I'm meeting and hearing more and more people share the same or similar ideas and desires. It's like "The Hundredth Monkey" effect. This is a time when more people are wanting to set up retreats or live in intentional communities. They want to share resources, live in nature, and work together, all to experience more health, healing, peace, abundance, and connection.

**Inspirational Autobiography**

People had been randomly telling me over the past few years that I had an interesting life and that I should consider documenting it. That idea planted a seed in the back of my head, though I didn't feel compelled to write a book until late May of 2021 when I received an email newsletter from Jan Edwards. She asked if it might be the time to write that book. I had received her emails before, but for some reason, this one caught my eye. This was the sign I needed. I was ready.

At the time I made that decision, and during most of the writing process, my desire was not to write a book for the public, nor to publish it, but to give it to my kids and my family and possibly others who expressed interest. I've not yet shared with my kids the information in this book. They will be learning things about me and them for the first time by reading this book.

When we reached the point that most of the first draft was written and I read through it for the first time, something in me shifted. I felt a higher call to get this information out to more than just my family and friends. If I published it and promoted it, and it did well, I could donate all the proceeds to my nonprofits, which could generate the momentum they needed to really move ahead. The book could bring my global community together and fulfill my passion to serve humanity. It was connected with everything else, the holistic oneness. Everything works together.

## The Perfect Storm

As I write this, it is the Fall of 2021. With the pandemic and global changes, people have been challenged beyond what they ever have endured before. They're confused. They've been thrown off by what's going on and their isolation. They don't know how to help their kids understand what's going on and know what will happen. There's conflict within the family. There's conflict in religion and spirituality. There's conflict politically. The conservative people want to talk about conspiracy theories. Kids and grandkids don't want to spend time with their parents and grandparents. Baby boomers are getting older, but have no plan for their final years. Their future is a dismal, dark, and unhappy place to think about. We have more polarization and division in countries, communities, families, friends, and relationships than ever in history.

We're in the fifth dimension where the energy is very dense and strong, much stronger now than ever in history. People don't know how to deal with all this kind of energy that we're being bombarded with. They're not grounded. If they're not grounded, they get thrown off. Then they don't know what happened. They wonder, *"Why am I feeling this way? Why am I not feeling good?"* Most people can't figure it out. They are looking for something right now, looking and grabbing, but they don't know what to grab or where to go. They don't know how to start or who to talk to, or how to reach the people who can help them.

All the elements make for a perfect storm. There's no better time than now for creating a new reality. We needed a major wake-up. We got one. Now, we need to work with it, for our evolution. We need to communicate. If we get enough people to awaken globally, we'll get to the tipping point. We need like-minded people to come together, to quicken the arrival of the tipping point, the hundredth monkey, so more people will finally see, *"Yes, there's good out there. Let's join them."* The timing is perfect for the things that my collaborators and I are talking about: Spirituality; The Law of Attraction; Ashrams; Health and Wake Up OC; The Hundred Year Tour, Plant A Seed Mentoring. This is a time when we need spaces like ashrams that feel like Heaven On Earth. People are looking for that. They're looking for safety, security, and comfort. They're looking for a haven of hope.

As I've gotten to know more people on the same wavelength (vibration) with the same positive intention to uplift the energy of humanity, I've felt an increasing desire to get all of them in one room to start talking, to come together, to have the conversation. I'm looking to bring together all of the talented, creative, and inspired people that I know—*and those I will come to know*—who want to contribute and create something new and better and positive. The one condition that I want all of us in that room to agree on is that the income is not for our personal benefit, but rather to support the charitable groups and nonprofits that we want to start, like The Hundred Year Tour, retreat centers, and ashrams. It's for uplifting humanity.

All of these very talented and inspired people just need someone to bring them all together in one room to share ideas and begin brainstorming. *I want to be that person.* I want to coordinate the meeting with them, to help them collaborate, to start creating new businesses and ventures. I want to see what we can generate on a daily, moment-to-moment basis, with the intention that *it's not about me.* That will weed out the people who aren't in it for the higher vision. But I'm only one person. We need a book or a show or a massive movement to get the word out.

When you donate to humanity, more things show up in your life. There's no limit to what can come out of that and what's possible. Like my sunset over Mount Fuji photo reminds me on a daily basis, *what we once thought could not be possible is actually possible.*

# Chapter 15

# Pruning With the Universe

*"Pruning is a necessary part of life.*

*In order to move forward, you must let go."*

Cheryl Richardson

Since the outside world has been opening up after the pandemic, it's also been opening for me. Things are moving more. More balls are in the air. I need to make sure that I handle all of them, or know which one to let drop. With all of the things I'm focused on, as each new connection, business idea, and venture gains momentum, I adjust my energy, my resources, and my commitments accordingly. I'm learning how to manage more areas now. There will be a little fallout in certain ones, including some of the groups that I'm involved in. I don't know how it's going to play out, but as my ideas and projects take off, I'll need to prune. That includes people I spend time with. My vision is high. I have to keep my eyes on the top.

This means that I act immediately when I'm inspired by ideas or introductions. It's easy that way, and it usually gives me something of value that I would have missed if I didn't act immediately. When I have a calling or an inspiration, I do it without thinking, instead of waiting or taking time to decide. I also don't think about how I'm going to do it. I don't come up with reasons why it might be difficult or not work. If I do any of those things, nothing gets done. Acting on my instincts, inspiration, and opportunities saves a lot of time and energy.

I also don't do it all alone. I bring other people into the fold to collaborate on my ideas and ventures, so they can take steps that contribute to the projects. If I don't have other people yet, I don't worry about getting things done. Some things get done. Some things wait. The things that want to get done get done. The rest wait.

I was asked how I do it all. As I write this, I've been here since one in the morning. It's the weekend. But weekends are no different from weekdays to me. I do the same thing regardless. I put a lot of hours in. The benefit of all the health devices and practices I use is that I'm able to go into a really deep REM sleep every night. So, I wake up fully refreshed and energized, and I don't get tired.

I'm always working to increase my level of energy, to raise my vibration. One way I do that is by working with the energy of numbers, like always listening to 369-megahertz music in the background of whatever I'm doing. Three, six, and nine are called God numbers. They infuse whatever I do with God energy. I use those numbers in anything I do, as well as any numbers that are multiples of three, like twelve or twenty-four. I swirl my energetic wine glass product, like you would a singing bowl, eighteen or twenty-one times. I even set the cruise control speed in my car to multiples of three, so, depending on the speed limit, I set it to thirty-nine, forty-eight, fifty-four, or sixty-three. I also work with the energy of eight, the number of infinity and power. That's why I swirl my arm in the infinity sign in front of my Mt. Fuji picture when I do my morning meditation.

From a muted child in Japan, to the uncovering of my Samurai ancestry and inner focus that has brought me peace, I have come to the place where what I focus on and everything I do is about how I feel, not external situations and people. For most of my life, I was a people pleaser. They say contrast brings new desire. I've definitely had the contrast and desire for spreading peace and love has been continually flowing in me.

I love my life and focus on what I'm passionate about. I'm learning how to readjust my time between work, spiritual learning, health and self-care, recreation and socializing with old and new friends, and participating in networking and other events. In trying to keep all the balls in the air in the balancing game, I'm learning new ways of navigating my movement forward that will feel good to me, without hurting anyone's feelings.

I just go with the feeling. And it doesn't have to be all positive. It could be negative, like I'm going to disassociate from a group of people. I always say that people will come into or leave your life, your company, or your group organically. You don't need to try to make things happen. You just tune in to yourself and hold that focus, and things around you will go where they will without your stressing or interfering.

I had been in the habit of getting together once a month for hiking and other things with childhood friends and new close friends I've developed. As I've grown and evolved, however, I haven't been spending as much time with them. A buddy I've had since elementary school and I don't really talk to anymore, because he's in a state of fear from the pandemic, and I'm not in that mindset. He always feels negative and talks with a victim mentality. I didn't have a problem staying connected with him before, but in our most recent conversation, I found myself not really wanting to talk to him. I'm no longer at the frequency that I used to be. I didn't have to do anything about my feeling, though. He began distancing himself from me because of my different views on the pandemic and the vaccine. The shift happened naturally.

Another friend, who used to invite me to holiday functions, told me that he didn't want me to come last year because of our differences on the pandemic and vaccine and the fears of other people who would be at the function. That felt fine to me. Even if he did want me to come, I wouldn't be able to find anyone I could connect with. We are so differently aligned. I would only be going as an obligation, which would feel strained and awkward.

The group of friends that I had estranged myself from said, *"Sam's too good for us now."* Though we're no longer estranged, I don't golf with them or meet for heavy drinking. If I did, they wouldn't make statements like that to me, but what they say about me doesn't bother me at all. I know what's going on. When you keep evolving, your choices of individuals and groups to associate with keeps evolving. The people you are close to keep changing. I have new friends and groups who align with me and support the person I've grown into. So, I limit visits with old friends like my golfing, drinking, and childhood friends to special occasions.

Friendships are like marriages. You get married because you enjoy each other's company, but the marriage splits apart when one person grows at a different pace, or in a different direction than the other. With the split, the connection you once had dulls or completely disappears. This same thing happens in a microcosm with groups of friends. You move away from each other, not because you don't like each other, but because you move to other groups and activities that resonate with who you are now and whom you are becoming.

These people are no longer in my space, not because I did anything, or left them, but because they separated from me. I don't agitate or stress over thinking that my former friends and connections might resent me now because I've changed. None of that even enters my mind. I'm finding that those friends and the people they associate with are superficial, or judgmental, or just ignorant. So, their distancing from me is working for me. I don't want to hang out with them anymore.

In expanding my connections with more people through networking, I'm meeting a lot of healthy and higher-vibration energy people, but not all are like that. I've noticed that many people who are strong manifestors are driven by strong egos. When ego-driven people get to a certain level in their accomplishments, their egos get reinforced, because they believe that their ego and effort got them there. At some point, they shift into doing what they're doing to keep the fire of their egos stoked, rather than from a pure heart space of wanting to help people. In some people, the ego never melts and, eventually, turns into greed. As I look at these kinds of people, sometimes, I want to ask, *"How much do you need?"*

I've been more keenly observing the new people I meet, to determine where they're coming from ego-mind or heart. If they're coming from ego-mind, I immediately lose interest. We're not resonating on a close enough frequency, so the connection eventually changes or breaks. I don't do anything to disconnect it. I just let The Law of Attraction do its work.

The universe organically orchestrates the disconnections. That's the Law of Attraction working. People organically distance themselves or leave when their frequency changes or is too different from yours. This includes family members. But all of this is affecting me in a beneficial way. I look at these changes as positive. They're freeing up my energy and time for the people and activities that feel good to me and that match my frequency, even activities that I do alone, without anyone.

Many people have the viewpoint that being alone is a bad thing. They don't understand how you can enjoy going somewhere by yourself. Someone recently asked me, *"When are you going to go on vacation?"* I answered, *"Oh, I might go to Sedona."* They asked, *"You're going by yourself?"* I responded, *"Yeah, I'm having a date with the Divine!"* How can you be alone if you're having a date with the Divine?

Doing things alone doesn't mean I'm hiding from something or someone. I could hang out with someone or have someone join me, but I enjoy getting away from computers and cell phones by myself to contemplate and meditate and continue my personal journey. I don't have to think about the reasons I want to go, or when I want to go, or where I want to go. I just go with what I feel, and it all evolves naturally. That's working with my inner self and The Law of Attraction.

I wasn't always this way. For most of my life, I was a people pleaser. I wanted people to be friends with me. I wanted people to want to be with me. I needed that validation because I didn't have an accurate or complete self-validation. I've gotten to a place where I don't need that anymore, and the universe takes care of me. Life just flows. The God energy I surround myself with gives me what I need to feel alive and happy and to do all that I want to do.

# Chapter 16

## Passion ~ Purpose ~ Path

*"Pay attention to the things you are naturally drawn to.*

*They are often connected to your path, passion, and purpose in life.*

*Have the courage to follow them."*

Ruben Chavez

There was a time when I thought my life purpose was drinking and going to bars and hanging out and having a good time. Some people think that their job, their role in the family, their life plan, or their karma suffering is their life purpose. None of those are what your life purpose is. Your life purpose changes as you change.

Life purpose is a big blanket that covers your essence, your gifts, your passion, your mission and everything you create from that. My life purpose changed a lot. As I've continued to evolve and connect to a deeper knowledge of how I can serve humanity, all of the connections I've made continue to expand and support me and my ideas. I keep growing, and I don't let anybody slow me down. This process is my evolution. This is all in alignment with my life purpose.

- To connect with new people of like mind, heart, spirit, and vision, to work together in some capacity, and stay on the same wavelength.
- To continue raising my level of total health, vitality, and vibration. It's hard to have peace on earth if you're suffering physically or mentally. You can't be present for yourself or anyone or anything if you're in a fight with inner demons.
- To develop my nonprofit organization, the ashram, the board and care facility in Japan, and The Hundred Year Tour, all of which will evolve and expand.
- To bring peace on earth—*or, like my yogi says*—to help others go from suffering to celebration.

If you ask me two years from now what my life purpose is, I may tell you exactly the same thing. Or it may be different than I'm able to perceive right now. I'm open to whatever the universe brings me. My path looks really different from ten years ago—even five years ago. But that's my path, to keep evolving. Looking back from where I came to where I am now, I can see that I'm on track.

# The Path I Walked

Muted

Athletics & Academics

Family

Accountant

Speaking

Holistic Work

Networking

Unmuting

Law of Attraction

Non-profits

Spiritual Expansion

Friendship Evolution

Frequency Rise

Product Creations

Collaborations

Future Visioning

Living My Purpose

Fully Self Expressed

# Chapter 17

# Reflecting and Defining Moments

*"The finish line is for the ego.*

*The journey is for the soul."*

Pattie Gonia

All of us have had moments in our lives when everything changed. I call them defining moments. My dad's naval ship was attacked, and everyone was killed, but he escaped death. If he hadn't volunteered to stay on the desolate island and forage for food, which probably seemed like the worst kind of sacrifice, he would have died. I would never have been born. The male side of my family lineage would have come to an abrupt ending.

I can see many of these defining moments in my life, when one thing happened, or one person said or did something that was a positive catalyst for changing the course of the rest of my life.

Here are a few of my defining moments.

- On my family's move to the US, my mom stopped being the stern tough mother I had known and allowed me to be freer. With this move to the US, I was also given the opportunity to grow up on a farm, receive mentoring from my uncle, learn English, and experience a completely different life.

- Talking to the life insurance agent during my junior year of college resulted in him comparing policies based on my career major and changing my career path. This enabled me to be stationed in Hawaii, instead of Vietnam, and lowered my risk of early death from a potential explosion in a lab working as a chemist.

- Disconnecting from my golfing buddies simultaneously saved my liver and initiated my triple journey into self-discovery, health, and spirituality.

- My compassion for my employee's husband's prostate cancer diagnosis prompted me to get a library card, which brought me to A Course In Miracles, which gave me lifetime friendships. It also completely changed my understanding of myself, God, the Universe, and The Law of Attraction, and began my spiritual journey.

- My spontaneous decision to participate in The Landmark Forum brought out my buried emotions and moved me to take actions that I couldn't take before. This helped me connect with more people in a more authentic and heart-centered way. It also prompted me to offer the program to my employee, which changed her life and gave her the strength to speak her truth and leave the firm. Leaving the firm provided an opening for my nephew to work for me, which also helped my other employee to do her job more easily, which saved my biggest client, which saved my firm.

- Joining Toastmasters was the catalyst for the beginning of my unmuting and my trusting that what I have to say is worth saying and worth hearing. It also opened my ability to speak to others to help and uplift them.

- Joining BNI provided many outcomes, including expanding my network of connections, some of whom became good friends and collaborators with my ventures and projects. One of these was the person who helped me write this book. My decision to publish it will not only inspire others, but promote my services, and expand my humanitarian nonprofits and all who will benefit from them.

- The synchronistically timed trip to Mt. Fuji led to my receiving many health opportunities and a painless, successful, and fulfilling trip. It also provided the Divinely timed thirty-second window for my daughter to capture the amazing sunset, which gifted me a sacred scene to hang on my wall that contributes to my daily inspiration and spiritual practice.

There are too many defining moments of my life to list here. And there will be more. They don't stop. That's the way my life works, just like contrast and new desires. They say that contrast creates desire. From every bad experience, you have comes a desire to have a different experience, to neutralize the bad experience. Through contrast, you get new desires. That's always happening.

It may look like you're making mistakes or experiencing tragedy until you change your perspective or give it time to transmute and produce something you weren't expecting. Mistakes and tragedies make you look at things differently. It's not that I welcome them, but if they happen, it doesn't bother me at all. I know that something positive will come of it.

If all the challenges in my life hadn't happened, I would never have become the person I am. I would never have met the people I've gotten to know. All the contrast and change I've experienced have created the ability to get into a space of understanding. When you're in a space of understanding, you have zero drama. There were definitely traces of drama in my past, so not having that anymore gives me peace of mind.

I've come a long way from the muted child in Shimane-Ken, Japan. I have no regrets—*about anything.* I would not change a single thing, because it's the combination of everything that's happened to me that created who I am today. If I went back in time and tweaked even one thing, everything would be different today. Every decision we make on our life path affects the person we end up being. I'm comfortable with who I am right now. I wasn't always that way. I've evolved and grown. I'm mastering my energy and integrating my parts. Some parts of me are unchanged, like giving, taking risks, and knowing when to be silent. But I am no longer muted. I know when to speak. I know what to speak about. And I know what place inside me to speak from.

Life is a journey. We all have similar experiences along the way. My journey is as unique as my DNA. I'm a deeply spiritual person, and my belief system is sky-high. The Universe and Source are orchestrating everything for me, as they are for everyone. That's the one experience that every human has in common. When we're in high energy, high frequency, and high vibration, good things are going to happen. When we stay in that energy, good things will keep happening. This is what my life is like now, and it's continually happening, even as I write these words.

# Chapter 18

# Seeing Self Differently

*"You can spend a lifetime trying to be One with the Great Spirit.*

*Or, simply focus on Love, and realize you already are."*

Anonymous

My wish for my kids is my wish for you—that this book has helped you to see yourself differently, and helped you to rise to a higher place where your perspectives are changing. Maybe this is the stepping stone you didn't know you needed to help you open yourself and expand your beliefs. I know that this book has planted a seed in you, a seed of inspiration and belief that you can create a state of joy, ease, and abundance in your life experience.

We're not just human beings. We are all God beings. It's hard for most people to understand what that means. It's hard for most people to say, *"I am God."* It's a bold statement. People feel that it's a sacrilege to say that. They don't believe that they are God, Source, or extensions of the Energy that created the Universe. Yet, Jesus said, *"You shall do what I've done, and even more."*

These are some of the phrases I use in my morning ritual. I recommend adding them to your daily thoughts, affirmations, prayers, meditations, beliefs, or routines. Try saying one right now. If it feels wrong or uncomfortable, set your judgment, fear, and worry aside, just for a moment. If it still feels difficult, maybe this is an opportunity to expand your study of spirituality and universal principles a little wider and higher. You know when you're up in a plane, how high and wide you can see? Just because you couldn't see all of it from the ground, or know it was there, doesn't mean it wasn't. You just couldn't see it from the low elevation.

If it actually feels lighter, or even a little daring to say these phrases, consider that as a sign. Open your heart. Be fearless. Take a risk. Life is an adventure. You're here to enjoy it. Open a new door to what's possible. Watch how your life begins to change.

"I am God."

"I am Love and Appreciation."

"I am Happiness and Joy."

*As much as possible, remember to*

"Be in the world, but not of the world."

~ Jesus

# ACKNOWLEDGEMENTS

First, I want to express my gratitude to my good friend, Pedro Lopez who introduced me to The Landmark Forum. Taking that life-changing course was the catalyst for my one-hundred-eighty-degree turn for the better.

I also want to acknowledge Jan Edwards, who, after meeting in 2013 at The Holistic Chamber of Commerce, continued to support me in the different directions I took. She sent the invitation that inspired me to write this book and guided me through the process.

I'm also grateful for my friend, David Rohlander, who was instrumental in connecting me with a variety of people when we first met years ago. He has continued to be a good resource for me in my non-profits and networking, and in supporting my ventures.

Last, but by no means least, I want to send heaven-bound gratitude to my two Course In Miracles friends, Daniel Enfield and William Ervin. Though they are upstairs now, they are responsible for mentoring my initial spiritual understanding and accelerating my development.

# ABOUT THE AUTHOR

Sam Hashizu is a holistic, heart-centered philanthropist on a spiritual mission to create peace, compassion, and community for humanity's evolution, through collaboration, connection, and contribution. His entrepreneurial spirit has led him to diverse fields of business and many business start-ups, such as water conservation products, biotechnology, nutraceutical, and many others.

As a Certified Public Accountant and managing partner with Takenaga, Hashizu, Jay & Co., Sam developed a hybrid accounting system, called Holistic Accounting, a full spectrum approach aimed at the organization as a whole. Inherent to its design, holistic accounting motivates and inspires allowance of natural change and awareness of each individual's innate abilities and gifts. If managed according to the principles of The Law of Attraction, this ultimately relieves stress, increases productivity and employee creativity, and easily meets company objectives.

From the cradle to the grave, Sam is a Renaissance go-to man for education and resources on a wide diversity of interests, including investing, trading, futures market, accounting, insurance, real estate, nonprofits, startups, entrepreneurship, networking, mentoring, holistic health, life purpose alignment, spirituality, and the Law of Attraction.

Sam lives with his wife in Irvine, California and shares his time between family, his accounting firm, consulting, speaking, collaborating, physical and spiritual care, humanitarian projects and nonprofits, and solo journeys with The Divine.

Owner/Consultant - Makeover My Life
Author - *The Unmuting*
Holistic Accountant
Managing Partner - Takenaga, Hashizu, Jay & Co. CPA

# CONTACT ~ CONNECT
# COLLABORATE ~ CONSULT

Takenaga, Hashizu, Jay & Co. CPA  www.thj-cpa.com/index.php

Plant A Seed Institute                    www.plantaseedinstitute.org

Divine Yoga International              www.divineyogaintl.com

The Hundred Year Tour                www.thehundredyeartour.org

Linked In:              www.linkedin.com/in/sam-hashizu-0a3b2b1b

Heaven On Earth Ashrams                  Website Coming Soon!

Board and Care Facility, Japan           Website Coming Soon!


Contact Sam
to
Connect Collaborate Consult


For information on Holistic Accounting, Holistic Business Management services, non-profits, collaborative projects, or a consultation on a specific area of interest, schedule time with Sam at: Theunmuting@gmail.com